# THE GABLE MAGIC

Here, for the first time, is the whole story
of Clark Gable—a fascinating, full-length
biography of the spectacular career and private
life of the greatest movie star of all time!

Follow him from his bare-knuckled days in the oil
fields and lumber camps to stardom in Hollywood!

See him in his most intimate screen moments
in the arms of the glamorous movie queens
from Jean Harlow to Marilyn Monroe!

Live with him through the ecstasy and tragedy
of his five marriages!

Know him as he waits for the birth of his first
child, only to miss the greatest joy of his
life through his own untimely death!

Here, in words and pictures that the fans
of Gable will never forget, is the true magic of
the man whose life was a legend, who lived
every fabulous moment of it right to the hilt!

George Carpozi, Jr. is the Night City Editor of the N. Y. *Journal-American,* one of America's largest daily newspapers. The difficult and exacting routines of his job have not prevented him from occasionally returning to the typewriter while he runs the city desk to turn out a prize-winning news story. He won the New York City Newspaper Reporters Association "Gold Medal Typewriter Award" for his stories that directly resulted in the arrest of the city's notorious Mad Bomber, and in 1960 was a winner in The Hearst Newspapers' National Writing Contest. In 1960, also, exclusive of his duties as a newspaperman, Mr. Carpozi wrote and had published 65 magazine articles and two full-length biographies. His writing specialty is Hollywood personalities. Critics acclaim him as "The Biographer of the Stars."

*Other books by Mr. Carpozi:*

THE STORY OF BRIGITTE BARDOT
MARILYN MONROE: HER OWN STORY

# CLARK GABLE

by George Carpozi, Jr.

**WILDSIDE PRESS**

# CLARK GABLE, *by George Carpozi, Jr.*

## ACKNOWLEDGEMENTS

The author is indebted to many dozens of persons who have furnished information and material for the preparation of this biography on the King of Hollywood. In particular the author wishes to pay special thanks to the following for their valuable assistance:

Head Librarian Paul Feis and the Reference Department of the New York *Journal-American;* Jack Podell, editor of *Motion Picture Magazine;* Pete Martin in *The Saturday Evening Post;* Hollywood columnist Louella Parsons, Jim Tully, Davis J. Walsh, and Eleanor Packer, representing King Reatures Syndicate; syndicated columnist Dorothy Kilgallen, the "Voice of Broadway"; syndicated columnist Louis Sobol, movie critic Rose Pelswick, syndicated columnist Igor Cassini (Cholly Knickerbocker), and Louis Reid, all of the N. Y. *Journal-American;* Hollywood columnist Sheilah Graham, Harry Altshuler, and Joseph Carter, of the N. Y. *Mirror;* Hollywood columnist Florabel Muir and Jess Stearn of the N. Y. *News;* Hollywood columnist Joe Hyams, of the N. Y. *Herald Tribune;* Hollywood columnist Sidney Skolsky and Norman Poirier of the N. Y. *Post;* David Balch of the N. Y. *World-Telegram & Sun;* James Lee, James Padgitt, Dixie Tighe, and Elwood Pierce, who wrote for International News Service; Robbin Coons of the Associated Press; Cameron Shipp in *Cosmopolitan,* and Louis Berg in *This Week.*

Much help was found in reference material and stories by the late Damon Runyon and the late Ernie Pyle; Adela Rogers St. Johns, and Josephine Dillon Gable. Also special thanks to John Pascal, of the N. Y. *Journal-American.*

The publishers thank the following sources for the use of the pictures on the pages indicated: top (T), top left (TL), top right (TR), center (C), bottom (B)

Culver Service: 37(B); 115(T). Eve Arnold—Magnum: 47(T). Paramount Pictures: 126; 127. Penguin Photos: 114; 116(T); 119(T); 122; 124; back cover (C). Pictorial Parade: 34(TL); 118(T); 123(B). United Artists: 48(T); 128. United Press International: 44(T); 115(B); 117(TL). Wide World: 34(TR, B); 35(T); 40(C); 47(B); 48(B).

Photograph from the motion picture "BAND OF ANGELS" appearing on page 125 copyrighted © 1957 by Warner Bros. Pictures Distributing Corporation.

*Special credit:* All other pitcures appearing on the covers and on pages 33-48 and 113-128 were supplied through the courtesy of *Photoplay Magazine* and Metro-Goldwyn-Mayer. The publishers gratefully acknowledge their cooperation.

First printing: *May 1961*

## Table of Contents

1   A Star Passes ........................................... 6

2   How You Gonna Keep 'Em Down on the Farm? ................................................. 8

3   Learning to Act ..................................... 18

4   The Nobody With the Big Ears .......... 28

5   The Stage Is Set ..................................... 50

6   The Second Mrs. Gable ....................... 54

7   The Gable Star Keeps Rising ................. 58

8   Long Live the King! ............................... 64

9   Woman Troubles ................................... 70

10   *Gone With the Wind* ............................ 79

11   *GWTW* Can't Stop Marriage to Carole ... 86

12   The Legendary Love of Clark and Carole ................................................. 93

13   Army Days ............................................ 103

14   Over So Soon? ...................................... 106

15   Marriage to Lady Ashley—a Brief Storm ................................................. 109

16   Second Wind ......................................... 133

17   And Then They Were Married .......... 142

18   "I'm Going Home to Kay and the Kids" ... 150

19   The King is Dead, Long Live the King! ... 157

20   It's a Boy! ............................................ 158

*Two picture sections will be found following pages 32 and 112.*

# 1

## *A Star Passes*

EARLY ON THE MORNING OF November 17, 1960, a pall darker than blackest night descended from the glistening, star-sprinkled heavens of Hollywood and transformed the film capital into a desolate, bleak city of mourning.

It was the day that Clark Gable died—a day that solemnly and sadly signaled the end of a glorious era which bridged the prodigious gulf in the history of the cinema between the early, frantic days of talkies and the present sophisticated times of the spectacular widescreen and the new generation of stars who inhabit the film firmament.

Clark Gable was a living legend for three incredible, unforgettable decades—decades that were dominated by his mastery and supremacy over the tinseled city of make-believe. He reigned as the undisputed monarch, as if he had inherited his right to rule from the divine powers that had bestowed on him the handsome face, the winsome smile, the muscular physique, and the sheer brawn with which he presided over Hollywood as "The King."

William Clark Gable, as he was born, was everything—he was simple, forthright, deep, quiet, thoughtful, neat, devoted, methodical, punctual, cautious, stubborn. That's a summary, by no means complete, which quickly frames a thumbnail sketch of his character and personality. But it hardly begins to scratch the surface of the legend that was Clark Gable— the man adored by millions of women who loved the overpowering spell he cast over their sex and admired by millions of men enthralled by his take-no-nonsense attitude and swaggering mastery over women.

Now Clark Gable is dead, and his death leaves a void in the motion picture industry that may never be filled, for Gable was generally regarded within the film industry itself as the best all-around actor of this or any other generation.

Vernon Scott, the Hollywood correspondent for United Press International and veteran observer of the cinema scene, summed up Clark Gable's talents in this keen and penetrating analysis:

"He played a man's man in a man's world as opposed to the Marlon Brando types who portray mixed-up, emotionally unstable weaklings.

"Whether it was drawing room comedy, romance, or horse opera, Gable attacked each role with the authority of a man of the world with an eye for pretty girls and a good brawl with the 'heavy.'

"The new batch of stars called him a 'personality performer' and frequently belittled his acting ability.

"But he won an Oscar in 1934 for *It Happened One Night*, and his performance as Rhett Butler in *Gone With the Wind* was one of the most memorable in screen history.

"Who then, can play Gable roles, sweeping ladies off their feet and eliciting sighs from the ladies in the audience?

"Can you picture Paul Newman swaggering into a saloon and announcing he can whip every man in the joint? Or Brando? Or Tony Perkins? Or Tab Hunter?

"Gable was one of a kind."

When Clark Gable died all Hollywood, all the world in fact, mourned him. Hollywood and the world have been saddened by the deaths of other heroes and heroines, but none was received with the genuine grief and heart-felt poignancy as was Gable's passing. For when Gable died there died with him a dream.

His dream. The birth of his own child. His son.*

When Gable was in Reno on his last film, *The Misfits*, all he wanted every day was to finish and get home with his wife, Kay, to wait out the baby's arrival.

"I'm taking off until the baby is born," Gable had told everyone when he returned to Hollywood. "No more pictures now. I want to be there at home and I want to be there a good many months afterward. . . ."

Hollywood's and the world's utter bereavement over Gable's death was expressed succinctly and accurately by director John Huston:

"That he couldn't have lived to see the child is the greatest tragedy of all."

Indeed it was a tragedy, but it's a better than even bet that Clark Gable himself would have been the first to express annoyance and contempt over the severity and sadness with which his death was received. For it was Clark Gable's credo to laugh at death, and perhaps nowhere was it better expressed than in the bit of dialogue from *The Misfits* which may well be remembered in the years to come by all who knew him as the way he wanted them to know him.

"Honey," the script had him say to Marilyn Monroe, "we all gotta go some time, reason or no reason. Dyin's as natural as livin'. Man who's too afraid to die is too afraid to live, far as I've ever seen. So there's nothin' to do but forget it,

---

* *John Clark Gable was born on March 20, 1961, exactly 123 days after the untimely death of his father. See Chapter 20, "It's a Boy!"*

7

that's all. Seems to me."

But the story of Clark Gable is not his death. The story is his life. . . .

# 2

## *How You Gonna Keep 'Em Down on the Farm?*

IT WAS FEBRUARY 1, 1901.

The snow swirled down in blinding, angry fury, whipping aimlessly in the brooding darkness of the early morning; the wind howled across the small, sleeping town of Cadiz, Ohio.

At two minutes past 4 A.M. Dr. John S. Campbell slammed the front door of the Gable house shut against the thrusts of the whining wind; he shook the snow from his coat, tossed it carelessly over a bench, and followed the tall, hulking man who had summoned him up the stairs to a bedroom.

As Dr. Campbell entered the room, he could see he had gotten there not a minute too soon. Lying on the bed, writhing as the pains came, ready to give birth, Adeline Hershelman Gable was looking up with silent relief at the doctor.

"You're going to be all right," Dr. Campbell said reassuringly. "Everything will go well, I promise you . . ."

Everything went well and at precisely 4:30 A.M. Dr. Campbell delivered Mrs. Gable of a bawling, blustery, bellowing baby boy who was placed in a delivery blanket cradled in the arms of his father, William H. Gable.

"He's a fair-sized one, Bill," Dr. Campbell observed a while later after he had attended the mother and started downstairs to put the newborn infant on the kitchen scale.

"All of twelve pounds," announced the doctor after waiting patiently for the wavering indicator to stop. "You can be proud of him. And, by the way, what are you going to name him?"

"Nothin' wrong with my name," the jubilant father blurted, "only we've got a different middle name. We're gonna call him William Clark Gable."

Dr. Campbell nodded approvingly and told the father he would make the appropriate entry on the birth certificate just as soon as the storm let up and he could make the trip over to the Harrison County Probate and Juvenile Court.

"How much I owe you, Doc?" asked the new father when

the physician was ready to leave.

"The usual," Dr. Campbell replied, ". . . ten dollars."

William H. Gable dug deep into his pocket and paid the bill.

It wasn't until much later, after the blizzard subsided, that Dr. Campbell went to the courthouse and filled out the data required on the document in the recorder's office. The delivering physician was precise in all the facts relating to the birth except in one detail.

He listed William Clark Gable as a girl!

The error was corrected quickly, but today if one were to visit the courthouse and inspect the record, the amendment that transformed him officially to male status can still be seen on William Clark Gable's birth certificate, corrected by a red line drawn through the word "female."

Clark was born in a simple home with simple surroundings. The house itself was not big, but it was adequate for the three people who occupied it. It had a gabled roof, eight rooms, a cellar, a small lawn and a short cement walk that led to the street. There was no sidewalk in the block in those days.

Those who occupied the premises were themselves simple people. William H. Gable came from Pennsylvania Dutch stock, as had his wife, Adeline, although she had some Irish in her, too. William Clark was her first and only child—a child she bore despite the doctor's warning that childbirth would kill her.

Adeline did die, when her son was seven months old, and this inspired one of the many Gable legends.

The story was that Clark was reared by a mean stepmother, that he ran away from home, and that he twice married women much older than himself because he suffered a mother complex. But, checked out through official sources, the "legend" takes on a vastly different aspect.

Left with a son too young to realize the great tragedy, Papa Gable was faced with the impossible task of caring for and raising the infant. He could not do it himself since he had to work, so he placed young Clark with his maternal grandparents, the Hershelmans, whose home was on a quiet Ohio farm bordering a lake. From his grandmother, he learned the principles of life that were to be his guide in the years ahead; that there can be no harvest without first tilling the soil and sowing the seed.

The farmhouse faced the lake, and there were no other houses near. His first few years thus were solitary and character building. Without the companionship of playmates, young Clark swam in the lake, watched the squirrels in the hickory grove behind the house, and the buzzards swooping down from the blue sky.

9

Each Sunday the old mare was hitched to the surrey and the boy accompanied his grandparents to church. They were Methodists.

But when Clark was five, his father remarried and came for his son. He brought the boy back to Cadiz to meet his stepmother, a gentle, cultured woman named Jennie Dunlap, who had been a milliner.

When she became Papa Gable's wife, she gave up her job and took over the full-time chore of raising William Clark. Jennie took an instant liking to the little boy with the crooked teeth, the wild mop of hair, and the jug-like flapping ears. She brought him up as her very own son, showering him with love and affection that quickly made up for whatever maternal care Clark might have lacked in the important first five years of his life.

Shortly after Clark's father brought the youngster home, the family moved to Hopedale, Ohio. There, as he began to grow up, he realized how lucky he was to have Jennie for a stepmother.

"She was a wonderful woman and dad was very lucky to have married her," Gable later said. "It was a lucky thing for me, too. She was a wonderful mother to me. She was like my own mother.

"After dad remarried, he spent most of the time away from home digging for oil and looking for the big strike that never came.

"Then when I was about seven my stepmother became ill. The doctor told my father she needed a quiet life. So we moved again, this time to Ravenna, which is about fifteen miles from Akron. We settled down on a farm and dad gave up oil-drilling."

Gable said he was a clumsy boy with "funny crooked teeth," but the kids never ridiculed him for these imperfections.

As a pupil in the elementary school at Ravenna, young Bill Gable, as he was known then, was a fair student. His best subject was spelling. He was also athletically inclined and baseball was his favorite sport. He played the outfield later when he attended high school and many, many years afterward Joe DiMaggio was to be his all-time baseball hero. Gable also played trombone in the school band, but never tried to act in the school plays despite one brief experience at it in his elementary school days when he played a little brown cuddly teddy bear.

When he reached the ripe old age of sixteen, Bill Gable had by then come to a crossroads of his life. On the one road he saw nothing more exciting than the future of a plowboy on his parents' farm; on the other he saw the huge outside world and its fascinating lures. Young Gable had reached a point in life where he had developed a desire for achievement and self-fulfillment. He could not see himself working or even managing a farm.

With his courage and self-confidence to strike out for the more alluring goals of life, fortified by the willingness of a pal named Andy Means to go along with him, Bill Gable packed a straw suitcase and made off into the world. And there was a box of sandwiches and a cake that Jennie made for them to take along in case the boys got hungry.

Leaving home meant quitting high school at the end of his sophomore year after having racked up a 94 in spelling and compiled a satisfactory all-around scholastic average with some 70s and a few 80s in his grades—he made a 76 in math, 77 in science, 77 in English, his major subjects. It meant, too, saying goodbye to his stepmother whom he loved dearly and to his father whom he admired and loved as well.

But Bill Gable was determined that somehow or other he was going to make good, somewhere, some way.

Bill and Andy headed for Akron where they promptly landed jobs at the Firestone Tire and Rim Company.

"I was casting around for something to light on," Gable related about those early days, "and I sure found it. They put me on a job of molding treads on rubber tires. It was a hot job for a young kid, but I learned about some things that make the world go 'round, and you ate through your own physical efforts.

"I was there for several months before I started running around with a bunch of fellows and naturally went to all the shows."

One night Clark went to the theatre where the Ed Clark-Lilly stock players were presenting *The Bird of Paradise*. He sat in the audience next to two young men whom he recognized as players in the theatre. They got into conversation.

"These actors on the stage," Clark said, pretending to be casual about it, "how do they get their start—do they have to go to dramatic school and study for a long time?"

One of the players, sitting beside him, answered that it all depended on the individual's talents.

"Some people have it, some don't," Clark was told. "A fellow could walk off the street sometimes and show the stuff that makes him a great actor. Others can go to school for years and never make it."

Clark began to think. He began to think of himself on the stage. Acting.

He was so excited he could hardly contain himself.

"I've seen you on the stage," Clark told the players, "and I wondered—I wondered if you think I might get a chance

11

to try out for something. . . ."

Just then the lights dimmed and the curtain went up. The audience fell into a deep silence and Clark didn't get an answer. He sat in his seat staring on the make-believe world behind the footlights, fascinated by the drama and the actors and the whole idea of being up there as a performer. What a thrilling life, Clark thought. How exciting compared with the dull routine of factory work.

Long before the final curtain fell, Clark had made up his mind—he would be an actor!

To his surprise, as they got up to leave, the players invited Clark to come along for a cup of coffee and a sandwich in a restaurant next to the stage door. There as they sat and ate, the other players from the Clark-Lilly company came in and took tables. In short order every word being spoken in the little lunchroom was about the theatre and about the evening's performance.

"If you're really interested in the stage," one of his two companions told Clark, "you can come backstage tomorrow and take a look around. There's always a chance you might get a small part—we're always losing somebody."

Clark's pulse quickened. His heart pounded.

"You mean it's all right to come backstage?" he asked incredulously.

"Sure it's all right," came the answer.

That night Clark Gable went home filled with an excitement he had never known. He hardly slept, thinking about the great adventure he was about to take—a visit backstage in a real theatre.

The next evening, Clark went to the theatre and met his new friends. They took him in and showed him around. They even let him peek through a hole in the curtain at the audience.

"I pretended," Clark said, "to be an actor and tried to get my reaction to how I would feel standing in front of all those people. They couldn't see me—but I could see them. I knew at once that I would not be stage-struck. It's strange, but I had the feeling that the theatre was in my blood. And I had hardly been inside the theatre then."

From that night on, Clark was a constant visitor to the theatre until all the players and the manager knew him. He would listen enchanted to their experiences and stories. Finally one day he got up enough courage to ask for a job.

And he got it!

The job of a call boy—without any salary at all!

But Clark loved it. It was what he wanted.

Soon he was thinking of asking for a small part. Any part, just so long as he could get out there in front of the footlights. But he didn't dare ask. Although his time in the theatre had been short, he had learned that valuable lesson, the unwritten code of the stage, "See and hear, but say nothing."

Then one night they came to him. They actually gave him a part. He was a voiceless extra, but he passed on to the stage—and that night when he went back to his room he dreamed of being Hamlet and Romeo and Cyrano and the great lover all at one time.

Still working at the factory days and playing the theatre at night, working for nothing, Clark did bit parts until one day they gave him the role of a butler to play—and what a butler he was! "Perfect" they told him.

Gradually his experience ripened. He played all sorts of minor characters in every type of make-up. All contributed to the all-important factor in the field he had chosen to make his life's work—experience.

And every part was a character role.

"I didn't mind," Gable said. "I wanted to play character parts. Funny how a young man wants a costume and a long gray beard. Every week I was a different character. But they were all walk-on bits. Used to walk on with a mop or a tray of dishes or something.

"I was paid nothing. And to be sure, I was worth every cent of it."

The year was 1918. Then came November 11th and World War I ended.

By now young Gable had quit his job at the rubber plant and gotten another in an oil refinery where the pay was better.

Not many months later the post-war recession hit Akron. Gable still managed to hold on to his job at the refinery, but the future wasn't too bright. He was still getting nothing for his acting.

Then one day a telegram came. It was from his father. "Come home. Mother is dead."

It was the saddest day in young Gable's life. He had loved his stepmother Jennie very dearly.

After the funeral, Gable returned to Akron and continued to work in the refinery and also enrolled in school. He had decided he would finish high school studies and perhaps go on to college. Young Gable had an idea he might want to become a doctor!

But a letter from his father changed all his plans. The elder Gable had given up farming and gone to Oklahoma to pursue his first love—oil-drilling. There was a new oil boom in the Sooner State, which was why the elder Gable had gone there to begin with. But there were opportunities in other fields, he wrote his son—like the theatre.

"If you come here," the letter read, "you'll be rolling in

dough. I can get you a fine job as an actor if that's what you want. All you have to do is come out here and see for yourself."

Bill Gable packed his bags and went off to Oklahoma with a glint in his eye and his heart full of hope. He was going to be an actor—and get to play those character parts he yearned for after all.

"Dad got me a job as soon as I got there—but not in the theatre," Gable said. "It was as a student tool dresser on the business end of a sixteen-pound sledge, twelve hours on and twelve off. I was twenty then.

"It was rough work. You have to heat the things to white-hot heat, then two men on each side with those sixteen-pound sledges start hammering on the face back. There's a steel gauge, and you have to hammer that back until it fits the gauge perfectly. Then the hole is always round and you get the proper size.

"So I began to learn what made that go. Out there where you're wildcatting you have to use wood, and we used to bring in great truckloads to keep the steam up. It kept a fellow humpin'. Every twelve hours the tool dresser goes to the top of the well, sixty-five or eighty feet, and greases the crown block. This was usually about midnight, and you go up with your grease can. Even in those early days I began to have a desire of wanting someday, if I ever made it into the theatre or the flickers, to make a picture with oil wells just like they were then."

Gable's wish came true many years later when he made *Boom Town*, with Spencer Tracy.

Continuing his story about his experience in the Oklahoma oil fields, Gable related that he was never too excited with the business of learning to be a tool dresser.

"But even though I didn't have my heart in it, I soon had seven strings of tools and got twelve dollars a day, and paid my own board. I slept in a tent. It was darn good money. But everything you bought there was about double price. Three or four bucks for a steak, and that in some joint."

Eventually the backbreaking job of tool dresser wore Gable down and he looked around for other employment, something easier.

"I found it at a refinery, but it didn't last long. They fired me. So next I worked on a labor gang. That was in the summer of 1920. It was a damned hot one. You'd work around those stills that refined oil, which creates a terrific heat inside the still. Every so often we emptied them. There's a certain amount of deposit, like asphalt, that settles in the bottom of the stills. You have to go in there and take that out. They let the boilers cool for twelve hours. You can stay in there for about twelve minutes. They time you. In two minutes, if you don't come out, they come in and drag you out. Then you sit out in the fresh air. In a gang of eight men you start work every sixteen minutes. We cleaned out storage tanks, too. You go in with a pick and a shovel and they tie a rope around you. One man would go in at a time. I don't know how they work it now, but then we'd work until we'd feel faint. It wasn't very long before you got hysterical. It was a very small manhole. Very small.

"I've seen lot of 'em in there a little hysterical. They'd start to laugh. Then they'd haul 'em out.

"I worked on this until February first of 1922. That was my twenty-first birthday. At that time I'd saved up a little dough, and my father and I had a little shack at the lower end of town. So I went home that night, my twenty-first birthday, and said to dad:

" 'I think I'm going to leave. I'm going to be an actor. I still want that more than anything else. So I'm going.'

"My father said, 'Stay here. I've got all these strings of tools. It'll pick right up.'

"Then he and I tied right into it. I told him I didn't want to work in the oil fields, nohow. I wanted to be an actor. Period. So, he ups and threatens me. He says, 'I can't believe you want to go into acting after all we've been through here. I'm going to tell your grandmother.'

"His mother was a real rugged old girl and I was afraid of her more than I was of him."

Clark turned to look at his father and saw through the anger written on his leathery face a tinge of sadness. For a moment, Clark was torn—should he stay, or should he leave to pursue the golden goals he hoped to reach. If he stayed, it would make his father happy—but his own happiness would be destroyed.

Clark turned his head now to hide the glimmer of a tear. At twenty-one, a man doesn't cry, no matter what he feels inside—and his father was not a man to countenance any signs of the "softy" in the boy he had brought up to be a man.

The words tried to find their way out but they wouldn't come for Clark. He wanted to explain things further. But he couldn't bring himself around. Finally, he managed to say, "I'll write, Pa . . ."

The words dropped off and Clark, still facing away from his father, waited to hear what he would say.

There was no answer, only a grunt, then footsteps.

Clark turned. The room was empty. His father had walked out.

"I figured that was a good time to leave—quick," Clark said. "So dad and I parted—not too friendly."

Leaving the oil industry to the Rockefellers, Gable headed

for Kansas City, looking for a start in the theatre. He found it with a tent show called the Jewell players, a cheap repertory company. His role? A general utility man.

With the company, which had about ten members, Gable toured the Middle West. In the summer they put up in tents. In the winter it was town halls and opera houses or anyplace that had a roof and a pot belly stove. Gable drove stakes, set up seats, played valet to the horses, and lipped the cornet in the parades.

Gable was quite impressed with the star of the show.

"I don't know where she'd been, or whether she'd ever played with Sir Beerbohm Tree. She was a one-eyed woman. Lost her eye fencing in a duel on the stage. But I thought she was a wonderful actress. Terrific. They used to do some Shakespeare things in the town hall if there was a university or a good school. They ended up in Butte, Montana, playing things like *Are You a Mason?*"

His persistence in becoming an actor finally landed Gable a role with the company.

"Naturally I ended up with the whiskers and all those things. I don't think I ever made over twelve or fourteen a week, and as little as two or three. There was no set salary. I even washed all the socks and sewed buttons on the costumes.

"Well, we finally blew up in Butte."

The show faded out of business during a blizzard in March of 1923.

"When that happened I was stranded in town with twenty-two cents in my pocket. I had two suits of clothes, an old, tired kit bag my stepmother had given me, a few sticks of grease paint, ties, and a shirt. I tried to get an acting job but there was none to be had. So I went working in the mines. The piano player was in the same fix.

"Well, when the twenty-two cents was gone, I hocked the bag. There was nothing to carry in it anyway. Bought a suit of coveralls, climbed on a freight train in that same month of March, and headed for the coast."

He was bound for Hollywood, but then again he wasn't. Gable wasn't exactly taking the straight line to Cinema City. His ride on the rods took him across the Rockies to Oregon, where he worked in a lumber mill for a few months, just long enough to stake himself to a job hunt in Portland.

"By that time I was a pretty husky kid. When I pulled out of Oklahoma I must've weighed 195 pounds or better, and I was all muscle from swinging that sledge. Of course, piling lumber didn't hurt either.

"The reason I went to Portland was that I had heard there was a theatrical job. This was a road company that played the lumber towns. So I hooked up with them. But we folded in Astoria, Oregon, at the mouth of the Columbia River. They were all fishermen, mostly Finnish. We played a week because we couldn't get out. So we gave up, and I was good and plenty broke again.

"So I ceased to act and went back to the lumber mill again. This time my job was piling green lumber. All the fellows worked by the foot. They worked hard. They made me work hard, too. Probably the toughest work I ever did. The logs were rough, of course, and heavy, and I had no gloves. They all wore leather gloves or a leather palm. I'd tie onto that lumber and it was like grabbing hold of sandpaper.

"I used to soak my hands. They had cuts in them and would be all stiff and crack open. I'd soak 'em up. Alum, too, that was the stuff. I had hands like a prizefighter until I got my first pay check and got my gloves, but I didn't use 'em before I got my hands all hardened up and toughened. After I'd been there about three months I forgot about the gloves."

Movie fans may remember the Gable hands—two hairy paws—which received featured treatment in a scene from *Gone With the Wind*. Women shuddered happily when Rhett took hold of Scarlett's scheming little head between those monstrous paws and said, "I could crush your skull between my hands like a walnut . . ."

And he could have, too!

Soon Gable had another stake and was on his way back to Portland to look for another acting job. But his money ran out again and again he was back in the woods. This time with a brush hook, cutting paths for a surveyor's team.

"You're a pathfinder. You carry all the tools for the engineers. Transits or anything. You put 'em on your shoulders and take off up the mountain with 'em. Ten hours a day, six days a week, and on Sundays you wash and darn your socks and do your knittin'. You don't go fishing or anything; you just sit down in the long house with a stove in the middle, with cots one right after another. Everybody slept in there.

"Your clothes are wet, soaking, and steaming, and you can imagine what that's like. Well, I stayed at that until it was finished. I had no place to spend my money. I'd saved a hundred and twenty-five dollars. That was a lot of money to me, so I went back to Portland and started looking for a theatrical job again.

"But it still was no dice. My stake started running low and I figured out a scheme for getting a job. I went over to the *Morning Oregonian* and talked to the editor about a job. I wanted to work in the want-ad department. That was my scheme. The editor sent me to the want-ad manager and he hired me."

The scheme?

Gable had figured if anyone was advertising for a man,

he'd be the first to know it. Patience makes a good fisherman—and in later life no one ever argued that Gable wasn't a patient fisherman. He got his training in the offices of the *Morning Oregonian*. Six weeks of it. Six weeks of waiting. Then came his first nibble. The Pacific Telephone and Telegraph Company wanted a timekeeper.

"That ad never got in the paper," Gable laughed. "I just went up and answered the ad and got the job."

The ad was the turning point of Gable's life.

With the money he made at the phone company, Gable was able to begin dramatic school. The year was 1924. And the dramatic school was operated by an aristocratic-looking woman of thirty-seven, a judge's daughter and a college graduate.

There is a story that Gable met her first at her home when he went there to fix her phone—he had moved up from timekeeper to lineman at the telephone company. But Gable always insisted that a lineman had no business going into anyone's home, so the story was incorrect. He actually met the woman who was to be his dramatic coach at her school in Portland when he went there to enroll in a Little Theatre group.

The coach was Josephine Dillon.

Miss Dillon not only took William Clark Gable under her wing as a pupil—but also married him!

# 3

## *Learning to Act*

AT MISS JOSEPHINE DILLON'S School, William Clark Gable was a studious, attentive, dedicated pupil. He was fascinated by his teacher's mature knowledge of the stage, for she had been an actress and had appeared on Broadway. Miss Dillon also had a degree from Stanford University, but the stage was what she knew best of all—inside-out. She taught her 23-year-old student diction and timing. She showed him how to sit and stand. And she found him a job in a local theatre.

They often talked about his chances of a career and Clark would say to Miss Dillon:

"Do I really know anything about acting? . . . Could I bring money into the box-office because people like to see me act? . . . Could I make people laugh and cry and go home happier because I was in that show?"

"There's a big job to do both mentally and physically," was Josephine Dillon's reply to Clark. "Learning the trade of acting isn't an easy one. It's a big one for you, Clark."

Hour after hour, day after day, week after week, month after month, Josephine Dillon worked on her pupil, teaching him everything she knew about the stage.

"Clark!" Josephine screamed at him one day during a hectic session that had lasted nearly five unbroken hours, "you've got to relax—you're not acting . . . you're like a machine. Forget what you learned in the stock companies. I am teaching you theatre . . . pretend you're talking to me."

Clark's eyes lighted up with anger. He stared at Josephine as if he wanted to leap at her and choke her.

"You're too rough with me," Clark said, trying to control himself. "What do you expect of me—miracles? I'm just a beginner . . ."

"No you're not a beginner," Miss Dillon raged back, livid with anger herself. "You're Clark Gable—I've trained you and I've sweated over you and you're an actor; you are good but you've got to be better. In my book you've got to be the best. You're almost ready for Broadway, but I want you to be more than ready—I want you to be great."

This was just one scene of many. Josephine was determined that Gable would make good. She taught him everything she knew.

Toward the end of 1924, Josephine Dillon and Clark Gable were in her studio and the teacher was talking to her pupil.

"Clark," Josephine said, "I'm closing the studio. I've decided to go to Hollywood and open a dramatic school. Will you come there after I settle down?"

Clark took his teacher's hand and pressed it affectionately.

"I'll follow you anywhere you go," he smiled.

Right then and there, the way Gable smiled, Josephine knew there was more to his interest in her than her teaching. And she herself knew, although she wouldn't admit it just yet to him, that there was more to her interest in Gable than the fine art of the drama.

There was a mutual desire for romance. . . .

This led to marriage on December 23, 1924—Gable then was 23, his bride 37.

It happened in Hollywood, shortly after Josephine had settled in the film capital and had been followed there by Clark.

What they saw in each other was a great deal more than people understood, or never understood. Yet apparently they themselves, Clark and Josephine, had both misunderstood or misinterpreted their mutual interests for the stage as the soundings of love. There was mutuality of spirit and an inner and abiding faith that both shared for each other that they perhaps thought was enough to bind them in matrimony. Time was to tell them they were wrong. But the year 1924 was not the time. Nor the year 1925.

It was early in 1925 that Josephine landed Clark—he had dropped the William now—his first job in the movies. Josephine was breathless when she rushed over to Clark to break the news.

"Ernst Lubitsch is making a picture with Pola Negri and Rod LaRoque—and I've gotten you a part," she said. "Just think of it! You're in the movies!"

"What am I going to do in the picture?" Clark asked in utter surprise.

"You're going to be a soldier," Josephine replied. "It isn't a great part, in fact it's a very small one. But it's a start."

Indeed it was a start. Gable showed up on the movie lot and sómeone pushed a heavy uniform into his hands, told him to put it on, and report before the camera. Clark did as he was told.

Later, when he had finished his stint and went home, Josephine greeted him enthusiastically and begged to hear how his first day in the movies turned out.

"They gave me a uniform, a very hot uniform," Clark related a bit disgustedly. "They also gave me a sword. Then they told me to stand in a certain place. And I stood."

He looked at Josephine for a minute, then asked:

"Is that acting?"

Josephine smiled. "Yes, Clark, you're in the movies now —and you're acting. Anything you do in the movies is acting . . . and, besides, you're getting five dollars a day for it!"

Clark finished his work in the picture after a few days but, to his great disappointment, there was no rush by the studios to snap up this unique talent. Gable came away from his first stint before the movie cameras several pounds lighter after what amounted to an all-perspiring performance.

Since the film studios did not beckon Gable with another bit part after his brief role as a sword-bearing soldier, he turned to the legitimate stage. Louis MacLoon, who was producing plays in Los Angeles, thought Gable had possibilities and promptly hired him for a production of *Romeo and Juliet,* starring Jane Cowl as Juliet.

Gable's role?

He was a spear carrier!

But he was on the stage. And he was getting thirty-five dollars a week.

"That was more money than I ever suspected was in the theatre," Gable said. "It convinced me that at least I was getting somewhere—maybe I was even on my way up."

He was on his way up, but it wasn't a rapid climb in those early years, the years of the Roaring Twenties. There were still many rough years ahead.

Years that saw Gable unemployed for long stretches between the closing of one play and the opening of another. In between, he pounded the streets, hounded the studios, chased down every lead to a job, even that of an extra. But still the movies were having no part of Gable.

He finally turned to the legitimate stage once more and landed a substantial part, the role of the reporter, in *Chicago,* with Nancy Carroll. It played fourteen weeks in the Music Box on Hollywood Boulevard, where every producer and talent scout in town had a chance to catch the performance. One producer was so impressed that he brought a contract offer backstage.

For Gable?

No. For Nancy Carroll, who immediately went on to stardom.

And Gable went back to pounding the sidewalks.

One day he heard via the grapevine that a stock company in Texas was looking for a second lead. Gable talked himself into the job. Gable was always a good talker. He picked up the knack playing those one-night stands in the Middle West, working with the glib members of the touring Jewell Players, some of whom were no better than shills. But shills are good talkers.

After a few weeks with the stock company, Gable suddenly was catapulted into the shoes of the leading man, after the latter walked out. This presented a new problem for Gable. He had studied diction, intonation, inflection, timing, delivery, and bearing under his wife's expert tutelage —but he had never learned the art of studying. Now that he had to fill a new lead role each week, he had to study.

"I'd go home to the hotel at eleven-thirty at night and sit till three or four in the morning. I'd count the sides—how many pages—and then divide into how many days; and I wouldn't go to sleep until I'd learned the quota for that day. Boy, that was tough. But after seven weeks it got to be easy. So now I thought I was a pretty good actor. But it didn't last. The company closed in May after a 32-week tour and I came back out to Hollywood and took another crack at pictures."

The year was 1927—the year the talkies came to Hollywood.

"It was still no go."

By now Gable began to feel that maybe he wasn't wanted in the movies. So he turned again to the stage. Fortified with his wife's encouragement and assurance that he would make a success of himself and by the confidence he gained in the

Texas stock company, Gable turned to the East and invaded New York. He hit the casting agencies, one after another. Within weeks he was on Broadway, playing with Zita Johann as "The Young Man" in Arthur Hopkins' production of *Machinal*.

"He is young, vigorous, and brutally masculine," raved *The Telegraph* about Gable in his debut on the Great White Way.

"Clark Gable likewise played the casual, good-humored lover without a hackneyed gesture," applauded *The New York Times*.

"Excellent as the lover," cheered *The New Yorker*.

Gable became an overnight sensation of the legitimate stage and *Machinal* had a reasonably long run, although it was not in itself one of Broadway's more enduring hits. There followed a succession of other plays after *Machinal* closed, but in these Gable appeared competently yet without distinction—mainly because they all turned out to be flops. *Blind Windows, Gambling, Hawk Island,* and *Love, Honor, and Betray* were the plays which failed to click for the outstanding showmen who produced and staged them—men like Belasco, George M. Cohan, Al Woods, and others.

On one of his between-shows trips to the Coast, in 1930, Gable made another assault on the movie studios. But they resisted as stubbornly as ever. Just then came a chance for Gable in the Coast road company of *The Last Mile,* and in he went.

The role was that of Killer Mears—created on Broadway by Spencer Tracy.

"I had gone to see it and decided I couldn't take the part . . . Not after watching Spence. I told the producer I didn't think I was good enough."

"You'll be all right," the producer told Gable. "You don't have to be so good in Los Angeles."

Surprisingly, it turned out all right. Gable was terrific. So terrific that Lionel Barrymore, who was in the audience, left his seat before the last act to go backstage and corner Gable in his dressing room. Barrymore had met Clark back in New York and was somewhat familiar with his talents as an actor.

"I'm going to direct a picture and I think I have a spot for you," Barrymore told Gable. "Will you come out and take a test?"

"I've had a crack at the movies a few times," Gable smiled, "but I never made it. I was just an extra."

"Well, I'm quite impressed with your performance here and I think you've got the stuff to make it. The big stars can't talk. I'm a director and I want to test you for a role I've got in mind."

"What's the role?" Gable wanted to know.

*"The Bird of Paradise,"* Barrymore replied, not knowing that he had just sent an electrical charge through Clark Gable's body. *The Bird of Paradise* was the first play Clark had ever seen, back there in Akron when he was a gangling sixteen-year-old.

"Okay," Gable said.

Barrymore set up the test for Gable with Irving Thalberg, who was head of Metro-Goldwyn-Mayer.

When he showed up at the appointed hour, Lionel told Thalberg Clark was the fellow he planned to test. Thalberg said, "All right, take him away." So they took Clark over to the make-up room and, with Lionel supervising, they put very dark make-up all over his body and curled his hair.

Gable chuckled as he thought back over the episode.

"Then they stuck a hibiscus behind my ear and put a G-string on me and took me down to the stage to make the test. I felt silly, but Lionel was watching and he said, 'It's okay. It's all right.' It must have been wondrous to behold."

Barrymore finally took the test to Thalberg, who took one look at it and said, "Good Lord, Lionel! No, not that. Take it away. Get out! Get out!" Lionel said loyally, "He's a good stage actor. He's young, but he'll be all right." Irving said, "Not for my money, he won't. Look at his big, bat-like ears."

"So, after my short-lived return to films, I went back to the stage for a brief time," Gable related. "Then along came a test for Universal and another for Warners in some of the characters I'd played in stock.

"They looked at the tests—and I went back to the stage."

Gable got into a road show that was playing up the Coast. He signed an eight-week contract with Louis MacLoon, who again was putting on the tour.

"MacLoon wanted to close after five weeks, but he had me under option to do pictures, so we made a deal. I would let him off his three weeks, and he would let me off the option because I had an offer now from Al Woods to go to New York and go into *A Farewell to Arms.*"

Gable was leaving for the train when an agent called him up.

"Come out to Pathé," he said. "Come running."

When Clark got there the agent whispered, "It's a Western," and the director said, "Do you ride?" But he didn't say what, so Clark said "sure." "Well, that's fine," the director said. "We aren't quite ready yet, but we'll start you on salary right now and notify you when we want you."

"That was my first jolt," Clark later recalled. "I'd been used to rehearsing three or four weeks without a salary.

"And they offered me seven hundred and fifty dollars a week. I never knew there was that much money around. I couldn't believe it. The shooting didn't figure to take long, and I could still go East for Woods and do *A Farewell to Arms.*"

Outside, after he left the director's office at Pathé, the agent asked Gable, "Can you ride a horse?" And Clark said, "I haven't been on a horse since I was a kid." The agent retorted, "How do you think you're going to play a hero in a Western if you can't ride a horse?"

Bill Boyd was the star and he was a good horseman. The agent told Gable he'd better get busy and learn to sit on a saddle.

"So I hunted up a riding academy and found a cowboy and hired him for two hours a day to teach me to ride. It was five weeks before they began the picture. By that time I could ride, but good.

"Meanwhile I had to solve a serious problem. I had an Actors Equity contract with Woods. Failure to keep it could have been serious, but I had been committed to the movie since I sat around those five weeks—three in Hollywood and another two on location—doing nothing and collecting that seven hundred and fifty every week. I didn't know when I'd ever get back to making that kind of money again.

"I called Woods and explained everything."

Woods listened, then said, "Go ahead and stay with your picture and I'll telegraph your release in the morning. Lots of luck."

"We finally got started," Gable said. "The location was in Arizona. The first day I was on that horse from nine in the morning till lunch, and I got back on him and rode till six. It was rough, of course—but for seventeen weeks at seven hundred and fifty a week, it didn't matter.

"I was a rich man when we were finished with the picture —ready to retire."

But Gable never got the chance to retire. Word got around that Gable, while not a very good cowboy, was decidedly a hit with the women. Metro called him in and gave him a part in *The Easiest Way*.

The year was 1930. It was the beginning of Gable's fabulous skyrocket ride to stardom. Even before *The Easiest Way* was half-finished, Metro put a two-year contract down before him and asked Gable to sign. Sign he did and thus began a long and incredibly successful relationship between Gable and MGM.

During all this time, Josephine Dillon had kept hounding and pounding at Clark with all the mastery of a great teacher; Gable's progress was proof of her success.

Their home life was simple and quiet, and when Josephine wasn't teaching Clark the finer points of the stage, they would sit and talk, if Clark wanted to talk. Generally they discussed acting and the great actors and the great plays.

"I loved those long talks and always tried to show Clark that it was just as possible to be great in those days of the late twenties as in any period," Josephine said. "History is something that is constant, not something past, and the history of acting must go on and on," she told Gable. "And you might as well be part of it—and you are!"

The story of how Clark and Josephine bucked Hollywood and gradually reached the plateau where stardom could be seen in the horizon is a story of trials and heartbreaks. Extra work. No job. Tiny parts. No work. Better parts. Again unemployment. Then good parts—and the first contract. Through it all, Josephine Dillon Gable was at Clark's side, step by step every step of the way.

Then, once Gable started to climb his Mount Olympus and the female hearts began to flutter at the handsome brute, the woman who was his wife began to experience the painful pangs of jealousy. At first she tried to tell herself they weren't real. But it became very serious after Clark began to get the better parts and was becoming a somebody on the Hollywood scene.

Josephine noticed it—every time it happened.

A girl who would wait at the stage entrance in a Spanish shawl . . .

A woman in a gold dress who danced, leaning too heavily on Clark, her arm too tight around his shoulder . . .

Another woman who fainted against the rattletrap Ford that Clark finally bought when he could afford the luxury of a car; the woman begging a ride to a conveniently distant home . . .

Women who invited him to tea to talk over his career and told him he should be *free*—free from Josephine and the strings of marriage . . .

Josephine also had the impression that a famous star was urging Clark to elope with her.

All of them, in one way or another, were offering what Josephine described as "female flattery and warmth and beauty—the eternal incense to attract the male."

Was it hurting Clark's marriage to Josephine Dillon, this sudden attention from women on every side?

"It was not fun to watch and to live through," Josephine said.

She tried to hold on to the marriage but she could see that her hold on Clark was gradually weakening. Their relationship began deteriorating.

Finally, the marriage between Clark Gable and Josephine Dillon hit bottom.

Clark and Josephine talked it over. They decided there was only one way out.

Divorce!

After five years and four months as man and wife, they were divorced, on April 1, 1930.

This ended the marriage but it didn't end the talk—the talk that went the rounds forever after when Clark Gable was discussed.

In all of Clark Gable's official studio biographies that were handed out over the years, only a brief mention was ever made of Josephine Dillon—and Gable himself never discussed his marriage to the woman, fourteen years his senior, who brought him up from raw lumberjack and roustabout and part-time actor to the threshold of movie stardom.

Whenever a reporter asked Gable why he and Josephine were divorced, his stock answer would be:

"You'd better ask the lady."

Miss Dillon herself was not always reluctant to talk about the divorce. Nor about the marriage. On occasion, she had given interviews and even written extensively about her life with Clark Gable. Her statements and stories invariably told about a marriage that was founded on mutual interests and mutual affection—but there was never a mention of the word love.

"Clark was really a grand person to have around," Miss Dillon said in one of her writings about her marriage to Clark Gable. "That means an awful lot in the tiny little places such as we lived in. Perhaps a great home is different, but I don't think so. There is need of quiet and mutual confidence in the minds of the occupants to make a peaceful home—it isn't the size of a house that does it. So we always got on famously. If he didn't want to talk, we just went about our separate duties, and if he wanted to talk, we talked.

"But what happened between us?" asked Miss Dillon. "Did he tire of his wife who was older than he, as the stories go—did he turn to the fascinations of younger, or richer, or more influential, or better groomed women? No—it wasn't that.

"I believe we were both lonely—and that the loneliness grew as we went on.

"I once heard a country grade school teacher tell of the hardship of her work. She enjoyed teaching, and enjoyed the youngsters, but the lack of adult companionship—the necessity of always talking down to the understanding of the scholars, or of the sturdy but uneducated older people of the community, became unbearable. She had come from alert city people who read widely and had an open-minded interest in all current activities.

"My life was something like that. After all, one must sometimes want to talk about something else than the husband's career! A few years difference in age can make a big difference in the point of view, but far more definite is the great divide between the thinking people of opposite backgrounds and ancestral tradition. As the saying is: 'that is something!'

"What went on in Clark's mind that did not concern acting, I do not know, have never known, and will never know—now. What did I think about when we were not talking about acting or his career? He never knew, and I have never known whether he ever wondered or cared. As for myself, I put in very little time resenting his silences, or in suspicions of possible other women—but I was often very lonely. Perhaps he was, too.

"I believe loneliness was the main cause of our final separation."

If loneliness was what Miss Dillon felt during her marriage to Clark Gable, her complaint could not be apropos after the divorce. For then Miss Dillon, or the former Mrs. Clark Gable as everyone referred to her, was never left alone for a moment by curiosity seekers, gossips, and chiselers of all kinds. Schemes of every nature were introduced to Miss Dillon under the guise of an audition for enrollment in her school. People would come to her continually in an effort to reach Gable. They had all sorts of schemes on their minds—insurance, gold mines, horse race bets, the numbers game, real estate. Always they offered to pay the ex-Mrs. Gable a commission, if she would only get in touch with Clark—or let them use her name as Mrs. Gable to back their schemes. But she always firmly refused.

Miss Dillon said many people often asked her why she took on her attitude of protection and wondered whether it wasn't for sentimental reasons. But her reply always was that there is a certain bond between people who have been married as long as she and Gable had been; that they had gone through certain experiences together.

Above all else, Miss Dillon was happy about Clark Gable's success and would never do anything knowingly to hurt it.

But Miss Dillon, despite her assertion that she was not sentimental, sometimes indicated differently. Sometimes she combined traces of sentimentality with bitterness, as exampled by this statement:

"When Clark had no clothes, no money, no grooming, no finesse as an actor or as a man, he had few friends, but they were real! But as soon as the gorgeous self that he learned to show began to be noticed, how the scavengers flocked! As soon as he had a car, and a good haircut, and a good dentist, and a couple of good suits—ah, how different.

"No, that is not fun to watch, and to live through, holding on helplessly and losing in the end—always losing in the end through inability to combat such weapons. Honesty and pride prevent that."

Josephine Dillon Gable insisted it wasn't all bitterness. She said there was contentment that came from the hard work that she put in with Clark because the work resulted in progress, and that brought the joy that comes from helping others accomplish their hopes.

Then the first Mrs. Gable finally added:

"And we ex-wives just smile and smile—God help us to smile!"

# 4

## *The Nobody With the Big Ears*

IF, IN REACHING THE THRESH-
old of stardom, Clark Gable owed his success to Josephine Dillon Gable, by this time his ex-wife, then the thanks must go to another woman for carrying him beyond the threshold into stardom itself—an unsung heroine named Minna Wallis, sister of producer-director Hal Wallis.

It was Miss Wallis who brought Gable to Metro's attention and enabled him to get his role in *The Easiest Way,* which led to his first contract. Here's how it all came about:

When *Painted Desert* was screened in Hollywood, a number of people noticed Gable and talked about his good looks and attractiveness to women. The bushy brows, the straight nose, the warm, infectious smile, the wrinkled forehead, the wavy hair all seemed somehow to add up to an overpoweringly handsome face; and added to these was the lean, yet rugged physique.

It all boiled down to one thing—he was a *guy!*

Minna Wallis was one of those who observed and felt the impact that millions and millions of other women would ultimately feel when they saw Gable on the screen. She went to Darryl F. Zanuck, then production head at Warner's, and told him he ought to look at Gable. Miss Wallis had done some legwork of her own and found out there were some tests Gable had made around the various studios. One was the disastrous scene from *The Bird of Paradise,* which had prompted Irving Thalberg, the boss at Metro, to blow up at Lionel Barrymore when the latter tried to sell him on his protégé. Naturally, that was not the good test, nor was it the one Miss Wallis had picked. Her choice was one that was at Universal—a bit done from Gable's stage role of Killer Mears in *The Last Mile.*

Those who saw Gable as Killer Mears on stage can never forget his superb portrayal. Vital, vibrant, virile, tigerish, terrifying, the stage rocked under the impact of his performance. The screen did likewise as the image of Gable filled the canvas with a physique of mighty power and a head and face that greatly resembled a boxing hero of the time—Jack Dempsey.

Why, you may ask, if he was so all-fired good, didn't Universal sign up Gable?

The answer appears to be lost forever in the clouded, misty events of the past. No one seems to really know.

Miss Wallis, who had seen the test, had it brought over to Warner's and called Zanuck to join her in the projection room.

"I have someone to show you," she said. "I think you'll go for him in a big way."

The lights were darkened and the screen leaped to life with Clark Gable, bigger than life itself. Five minutes later, with the lights on again, Miss Wallis turned to Zanuck and asked, "How did you like him?"

"His ears are too big," replied Zanuck. "Can't see him."

"But he's a wonderful actor—and so good-looking," Miss Wallis protested.

"Maybe so," Zanuck retorted, "but I still say the ears are too big. He looks like he's ready to take off like a plane."

Undismayed by the turndown, Miss Wallis headed over to MGM and collared Irving Thalberg.

"Have you heard of Clark Gable?" Miss Wallis asked.

"Yeah, I think I have," the studio boss replied, "seems we gave him a . . . a tes . . . OH!"

Thalberg stared at Miss Wallis incredulously as the index cards in his memory flipped up recollections of a young actor garbed in G-string and hibiscus over his ear, crawling mysteriously through a jungle looking for a girl.

"Why do you ask?" Thalberg said very cautiously, as if guarding himself against a trap.

"Because I wanted to know if you'd heard of him." Miss Wallis said quietly, puzzled by Thalberg's reaction. "I saw him in *The Painted Desert* and he was very good. I thought you might be interested in him . . ."

"Oh no, you don't," Thalberg yelled, "you're not going to sell me that guy—not Clark Gable. I've seen him. He isn't even a good native boy. And what's more—his ears stick out like a couple of megaphones. No thank you."

Miss Wallis was better prepared to cope with the ear bit. She had thought about it and had the answer ready.

"What kind of a director are you?" she said. "You know better than I that you can do wonders with the right kind of lighting and proper camera angles, don't you? I'm a woman and I tell you that he's really *something*."

"Maybe he is," Thalberg shot back, "but you're not going to get me to see *The Bird of Paradise* again—never again!"

Miss Wallis smiled. Thalberg was beginning to thaw. Just a little. She saw her opening.

"Then you will see it if I tell you there's another test. A good test of Clark Gable?"

Thalberg shook his head resignedly and mumbled, "Yeah, I guess so."

"Then come with me into the projection room," Miss Wallis said triumphantly.

Miss Wallis had the test all set up in the room.

The lights were turned off and Gable came on the screen in his powerful five-minute portrayal of Killer Mears.

Thalberg sat through the performance absolutely motionless, his eyes transfixed on the screen. Miss Wallis, peeping out of the corner of her eye, could see the director's intense concentration on the actor's movements. She smiled to herself.

Then, with all but the last few feet of the film remaining to be run off, Miss Wallis asked impatiently, "How did you like him?"

"I'm surprised," Thalberg responded. "He's all right. He's . . . well, he's good!"

"See," Miss Wallis said joyfully. "I knew you'd like him . . ."

"But I still say," Thalberg interrupted, "that his ears are big." Then he quickly added, "But I think we can fix those up."

In a few days, Thalberg summoned Gable to the studio. By then, Thalberg had had a meeting of producers and lighting experts, had shown them the *Last Mile* test, and asked for their thoughts on how to solve Gable's ear problem. They agreed that proper lighting techniques—especially softer lighting—and three-quarter camera angles would reduce the prominence of the handles considerably.

When Gable walked into. Thalberg's office, the room vibrated with the visitor's presence. He stood erect, shoulders back, chest out. A polite smile creased his face and his gaze was fixed intently on Thalberg. Gable made an immediate impression. Everything about him spelled confidence. Thalberg liked what he saw at once.

"Sit down," he invited. "You have come here highly recommended. I have a part for you in a picture we're starting very soon. It's called *The Easiest Way*. Do you want it?"

Gable didn't have to be asked twice. The star of the film was to be Constance Bennett.

In a week, Gable was given the script. In another week, production got under way after hurried wardrobe fittings. In those days movie productions were fast-paced. Most movies were shot in days, or weeks at most. There were none of the elaborate, intricate preparations that go into film-making today, with the shooting taking months and the financing running into astronomical millions. Of course time was taken with some films and a great deal of money was spent on those; but in 1930 the demand for movies was so great that the studios were churning out films on a production-line basis. No sooner was one movie finished than another one was rushed into the works. They spun off the studio sound stages with an almost narcotic monotony.

Mid-way through *The Easiest Way*, Gable was called into Thalberg's office. By then Thalberg had received reports on his big-eared actor's abilities before the camera—and had also caught some of the early rushes of the film. Thalberg was pleasantly surprised to find that softer lighting and judicious cinematography kept Gable's ears from upstaging their owner as well as the others in the cast.

"Clark," began Thalberg, "we like the way you're going and we've decided to sign you up. How do you feel about joining the family here at Metro?"

Gable swallowed hard.

"Mr. Thalberg, I like it just fine. Those words are music to my ears."

Thalberg glared at Gable, wondering whether that was a pun.

"We won't talk about your ears," Thalberg smiled, "but we'll say something about your salary. We've decided on six hundred and fifty a week. How does that strike you?"

Gable swallowed hard again.

"You won't get any argument from me, sir," Gable said.

The contract was signed in January of 1931.

Before the next January had rolled around, Gable had earned every penny of his six hundred and fifty a week. He made twelve pictures that first year! There were times when he was working on two films simultaneously!

Suddenly Hollywood and the whole country had discovered a new type of hero—a rough-and-tumble guy who cut through the pink icing of Hollywood glamor with his natural devil-may-care ways, the ways of a Middle West farmer boy, a rubber plant worker, an oil field worker, a roustabout, a bum, a lumberjack.

While most of the films turned out that first year were inconsequential things, *The Easiest Way* stood out, as did another, *Dance, Fools, Dance*, starring Joan Crawford.

In nearly all his films, Gable was cast as a lovable heavy who would manhandle the woman—then wait for her to apologize. Letters from fans poured into the studio from all over the country. They were wild about Gable. But it wasn't until *A Free Soul* that Gable scored his first great personal triumph. In this film, Thalberg cast Gable with the great Norma Shearer and the unsurpassed Leslie Howard. By doing this Thalberg signified that he had immense confidence in Gable.

Norma Shearer was Thalberg's wife!

The year was still 1931.

When filming got under way on *A Free Soul*, the Gable personality, for some inexplicable reason, suddenly began to project itself as never before. Perhaps it was the confidence he had gained by now. Perhaps it was the experience he had acquired before the cameras in the whirlwind pace of a dozen film productions in one year. Or perhaps it was the co-star, the beautiful and talented Norma Shearer, as thorough a professional actress as Hollywood had seen.

One morning during the shooting, Lionel Barrymore dropped over on the set to see how Gable was coming along. Suddenly Barrymore stopped dead in his tracks. His mouth opened. He squinted across the glare of lights to a corner of the stage where the lighting was a bit more subdued. The crews were setting up their cameras there.

Barrymore caught sight of his young friend, Clark. He was holding a woman in his arms. It was Norma Shearer. They were going through one last rehearsal before they would go on-camera. When Gable spotted Barrymore, he relaxed his grip on Miss Shearer and flipped the astounded Lionel a casual salute—as if the business of making love to the great Shearer was simply nothing, as if he made love to great actresses as a matter of routine, like eating breakfast.

"He was like a lean and hungry Jack Dempsey," Barrymore said. "His quarry, of course, was prettier. But you'd never know it from the casualness with which Clark handled her. He took it all for granted. I really had to admire him."

But the Gable personality did not please everyone as it zoomed onto the celluloid of the daily rushes. An unnamed executive at Metro discovered Gable was stealing the scenes from Miss Shearer, Howard, and even Barrymore, who also was in the picture. Barrymore, of course, was delighted. He was all for Clark, rooting for his success all the way.

But the front-office executive decided Gable must not be allowed to dominate the great Shearer and Howard. So he plotted out a scene that he thought would make the audience despise Gable, even if he did steal most of the picture from the ranking stars.

The idea was for Gable to slap Miss Shearer in one of the scenes. Of course, it was to be a movie slap. A light tap but a lot of noise to lend realism via sound effects.

But there was no need to phony up this scene. It came across with an impact far beyond the executive's expectations. Even Miss Shearer was surprised. Perhaps shocked would

# CLARK GABLE

**The Life
He Lived
The Women
He Loved**

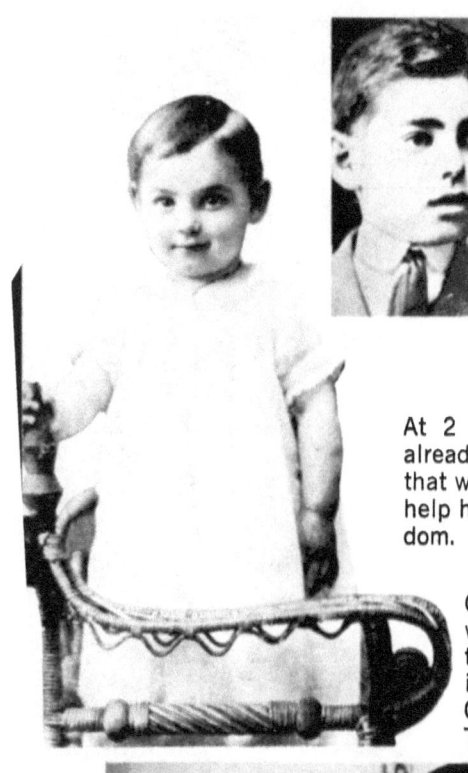

At 2 and at 12, his face already showed the features that would, in his early 20's, help him on his way to stardom.

Clark's father was a wildcat oiler and he tried to get his son into that work. But Clark wanted acting. They stayed best pals.

Clark's first wife, Josephine Dillon, was 14 years older than he was. She was a drama coach, taught him the art of acting.

Second wife, socialite Rhea Langham, taught him social graces.

When he started in films, Clark had no mustache (above) but when he returned to New York as a star (left) the "bristle" was a Gable trademark.

Expert barbering kept mustache in fine trim.

CH YOUR STEP

36

Earliest Gable rooter, Lionel Barrymore admires Clark's "Oscar" awarded for **It Happened One Night.**

Clark almost turned down the part of Rhett Butler in **Gone With The Wind.** Later, it became his favorite role.

Carole Lombard was Clark's third wife. Their wacky doings and their deep love became a Hollywood legend.

Clark caught this "cute" cougar cub on a hunting trip, and tried to give it to Carole as a present. Not surprisingly, she wouldn't take it!

Clark and Carole lived on a farm and loved it. Clark did everything — even the plowing.

After Carole Lombard's tragic death, Clark joined the Air Force (top) in World War II. He saw action as tail gunner in Europe (center), and had plenty of tales to swap with fellow volunteer Jimmy Stewart.

A sportsman all his life, Clark was equally at home duck hunting or fishing because the love of the great outdoors was in his blood.

The fourth Mrs. Gable was Lady Sylvia Ashley. But domesticity, and hunting trips, were not her cup of tea. It ended in divorce.

Making movies on location was always an adventure for Clark. **Mogambo,** top and center, was made in Africa. Clark always insisted on doing his own stunt work, roping, fighting, in films.

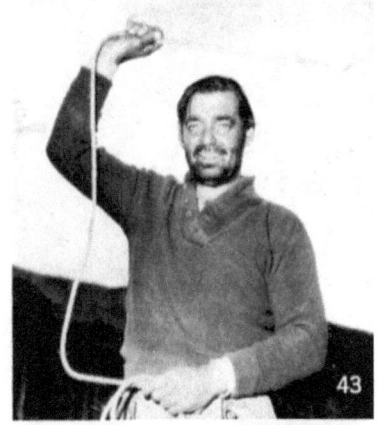

43

Skiing was Clark's favorite winter sport. His companions on this slope were Ingrid Bergman and Gary Cooper.

Many of Clark's friends were as famous as he was. Coop was one of his closest pals, another was Robert Taylor.

Between marriages, Clark dated many women. Some, like Virginia Gray (top) and Anita Colby, hoped he'd marry them—but he didn't.

Kay Spreckles was Clark's fifth wife—and the one who, many friends felt, brought him the most happiness. Their five years of marriage gave Clark the joy of family life he'd never had before.

Clark loved his role of stepfather to Kay's two children. Later, when Kay became pregnant, they waited contentedly for the birth of their baby.

Marilyn Monroe was Clark's last co-star in the long list of his glamorous leading ladies. They spent many hours together while on location for **The Misfits.**

Kay pays final respects to Clark at cemetery as Spencer Tracy and Robert Taylor mourn beside her. Burial was next to Carole Lombard.

be a better word for it.

Gable delivered a bona-fide sockeroo that rocked Norma almost off her feet.

When the movie was previewed the audience cheered with delight—women and men alike. Women sighed languorously over the caveman approach and the men, hearing the gals sigh, rushed to their mirrors to practice the proper manner in which to swat their lady-loves. It was a great moment in the history of films, for with that slap Gable knocked into limbo the smooth and courtly Valentino school of hand-kissing elegance. Suddenly Gable had given villains an unprecedented popularity.

Even Miss Shearer—despite the bruising blow to her dignity—was impressed by the slap.

"He was the most despicable of heavies, but even when he slapped my face you couldn't help liking him," she remarked.

Overnight, Gable's fame rocketed, and with each new picture he rose to still loftier heights. His star at last had caught fire in the Hollywood heavens, burning brighter, more brilliantly than any other.

Dimpled schoolgirls, dreamy housewives, gay grandmas turned out in ever-increasing numbers to form admiring, unruly mobs that surrounded Gable wherever he went. He became the central figure in the love dreams of millions of yearning women. Letters cascaded into the studio's mailbags from pleading women who cried, even begged to be slapped around by Gable.

"They had me clouting every leading lady after that," Gable explained it. "I didn't care, nor did I mind it. I simply laughed at the whole thing. I was making good money and I did as I was told. The only actress I didn't clout was Garbo. I guess if I had whacked her she would have clipped me right back."

Despite the excitement and near-hysteria visited on American womanhood by the new phenomenon of the silver screen, the country's males failed to be aggravated or angered by the undying female adulation heaped on Gable. They accepted Clark as a man among men, a man who could handle women the way women should be handled. They went for him in a big way, too.

Gable, moving now like a hungry panther on a rich and readily-digested diet of accolades, became Everyman's idol.

But while the world and its women were throwing themselves at Clark Gable's feet, none but two of the world's women really figured to any degree of prominence in Gable's personal life.

One was his ex-wife, Josephine Dillon Gable, whose acting studio had become one of Hollywood's most successful, where students were plunking down thirty-five dollars an hour to learn the knack of dramatics from the woman who was being hailed as the one who made Clark Gable what he was.

In one of her rare public statements, Miss Dillon was quoted as saying that Gable had told her when they were divorced that he wanted to marry another woman, a wealthy divorcee from Texas.

All at once everyone began asking who the other woman was.

And before long the answer would come.

The answer would come because this was Hollywood, the citadel of a flourishing industry which was so different than any enterprise anywhere in the world.

Clark Gable was one of those Hollywood figures now, and his life, for the most part, had to be an open book—and if he was in love with another woman, if he was going to be married again, the world wanted to know.

This was not the "old" Hollywood anymore, the Hollywood of silent films, but a new Hollywood, at the dawning of a new and glorious era . . .

# 5

## *The Stage Is Set*

WHEN THE TALL, SWAGGERING figure of Clark Gable descended on the Hollywood scene in the frantic, confused days of the late twenties, the motion picture industry was desperately hungry for a new male star— a Great Lover to succeed the Valentinos, Gilberts and Bushmans whom age, death, and the advent of sound had driven from the screen.

Then enter Clark Cable. Gable smiled the Gable smile, lifted the Gable eyebrow, and became the lover and landlord of Hollywood for the next thirty years.

Call it historic accident, but the fact is that Clark Gable hit Hollywood at a time when Hollywood needed another new hero in the grand tradition of a Barrymore or a Valentino. Whether another actor might have accomplished it is an academic question. Gable was there and with his unique attributes, he filled the void.

A corollary question is, of course, what caused the void in the first place? And the answer is not that a particular individual star happened to diminish at a given point in time and left a raw, hungry demand for another, but that the industry allowed that curious, unparalleled phenomenon called the "star" to develop at all. Certainly in the cradle days of moviedom there were no such animals as "stars"—those individual personalities stamped with the forever indefinable but always magic quality to grip the imagination and hold it. It was only much later that the "star" developed. In the beginning, actors and actresses were rarely given screen credits, and, even more peculiar, they didn't particularly want them. There was no real acting involved in those early one-reelers and any legitimate actor or actress who appeared in them felt vaguely uncomfortable, almost embarrassed as though they were somehow desecrating their great art.

What changed it all? Money. Money channeled through the sacred temple called box-office. It didn't take long for the performers to realize that what the customers were paying to see was not the story on the screen or even the novelty of pictures that actually moved, but instead this actor's handsome face or that actress' svelte, sexy figure. And with that realization came the canny, if inevitable conclusion that with the salaries of $40 a picture they were getting grossly and fantastically short-changed.

The producers, of course, had to yield. Reluctantly, at first, they gave the performers more and more money, but in time, even the reluctance vanished. Primarily businessmen, the producers realized the enormous wealth potential of a picture if its leading man was the favorite actor of the day. And in order to exploit the actor's drawing power to the fullest, the producers began splashing his name both in the advertisements and in the screen credits.

It drew the audience, all right, but it also added that much more lustre to the actor and his reputation—and, naturally, upped his price for performing. Nevertheless, it became the standard way to do things in the movie industry—producers even began bidding against one another for a particular performer—and that's the way the "star system" was born.

Charlie Chaplin, with his flapdoodle walk, his rolling eyes, his impish grin, his droopy pants, and his everlastingly present derby, endeared himself to the nation, first in the Keystone Cop series and later in such silent classics as *The Cure, Easy Street, The Pawnshop, The Immigrant, A Dog's Life, The Pilgrim, Sunnyside,* and perhaps his most famous of all, *The Kid.*

But other giants of the voiceless screen were blazing their own pioneer trails in the aborning movie industry.

There was William Boyd, who, before he reached greater fame as Hopalong Cassidy in sound pictures, stirred millions in his celebrated film, *The Volga Boatman.*

There was Francis X. Bushman of the near-classic profile, a matinee idol during the teens and early twenties, and one of the great Romeos in *Romeo and Juliet*.

There was the unparalleled character actor Lon Chaney, the man of the thousand faces. And there were still others, no end of them.

Douglas Fairbanks leaped and fought his way through the exotic fantasies that became his trademark.

Warner Baxter, George Arliss, Ramon Novarro, John Gilbert, and scores of others, and of course, there was the incomparable Latin lover, Rudolph Valentino.

Valentino, an Italian baptized Rodolph Alfonzo Rafaelo Pierre Fillibert Guglielmi di Valentine d'Antonguollo, scorched America's imagination with his torrid love scenes with the vampish Nita Naldi and strode across his tragically brief years in such historic movie landmarks as *The Four Horsemen of the Apocalypse, Blood and Sand* and *The Sheik*. Alone, he converted the Latin type from the brutal cad to the great lover and when he died in 1926, 100,000 weeping, sobbing, hysterical women lined the funeral route.

Along with the great actors, of course, came the great actresses. And one of the earliest was a fetching, dark-haired little thing out of Cincinnati named Theodosia Goodman. A braintruster at the Fox Studios, figuring to publicize her as an illegitimately-born exotic Egyptian, took the words Arab Death, toyed around with them, and came up with the anagram "Theda Bara." She swept to fame overnight in a film called *A Fool There Was*, based on Rudyard Kipling's *The Vampire*. It was no sooner on theatre screens throughout the land when "Vampire" was abbreviated to "vamp" and came to mean a female creature of prey. She played a great number of non-vamp roles, but it is as the Great Vamp that Theda Bara is remembered—for her siren roles in such pictures as *Cleopatra, Camille, Salome,* and *DuBarry*.

There were others as great and famous as Theda Bara. Pearl White was one of them, the always pursued, always fleeing Pauline in the memorable series *Perils of Pauline*.

Janet Gaynor, Mary Pickford, Marie Dressler were rising young stars in the silent films and so were Alice White, Louise Brooks, Sally O'Neill, Mae Murray, Dorothy Mackaill, Corinne Griffith, Florence Vidor, Phyllis Haver, Estelle Taylor, Aileen Pringle, Norma and Constance Talmadge, and Dolores Costello—and the incomparable IT girl, Clara Bow, the flaming flapper who made the boys sit up and notice.

In 1927, an episode of epochal proportions took place in New York City and then and there, the motion picture industry underwent the most violent change in its history.

The Warner brothers, Harry, Jack, and Albert, displayed in their Warner Theatre on the Great White Way a picture called *The Jazz Singer*, starring Al Jolson and May McEvoy, a revolutionary film that introduced synchronized sound on some portions of the same movie track.

The talkies had arrived!

The public's response was phenomenal. A great roar rose from the multitudes for more, and a year later, the Warner brothers followed it up with *The Lights of New York*, the first all-talking picture.

A new era—the era that exists today—was under way. Once the talkies were demonstrably successful, the public's appetite for them soared and the days of the silent movies were ended.

As sight blended with sound, a whole new generation of actors and actresses developed.

New names arose—Jean Harlow, Greta Garbo, Marlene Dietrich, Spencer Tracy, James Stewart, Gary Cooper, Bing Crosby, Tyrone Power, Errol Flynn, Alice Faye, Joan Blondell, John Wayne, and scores upon scores of others.

A new kind of film came into being since sound could produce subtleties that were absent before—sophisticated comedy.

With sound, the stars became bigger than ever, salaries rose to fantastic heights, and Hollywood went Hollywood in a great big way with actors and actresses leaping into extravagant homes with swimming pools and acres and acres of land and becoming party-givers extraordinary.

In time, new processes came along to improve films—3-D, and Cinemascope, and other processes that flooded the stages of theatres with gigantic motion picture murals that gripped the audience with the feeling that they were there in the picture with the stars.

Soon Hollywood was a Goliath in the rankings of industry in America. The influences of Hollywood spread to other countries and in the film capitals of each foreign nation the techniques and the modus operandi of our own cinema city became a pattern to follow—and copy.

And through it all—there was a King of Hollywood.

He was a unique creature of the cinematic firmament, a man who stood out among all others as the actor's actor, the film world's legendary hero who stirred the imaginations of millions upon millions of movie fans throughout the entire world; he was the King.

He was the one and only, the incomparable Clark Gable!

# 6

## *The Second Mrs. Gable*

JUST AS CLARK GABLE'S STAR began shining with unmatched brilliance in the heavens of Hollywood and a nation sat up to take notice of the screen's handsome new leading man, he sneaked away unannounced one afternoon during a busy movie-making schedule to Santa Ana, just southeast of the film capital, to attend a civil marriage ceremony. The bride was 41-year-old Maria Rhea Franklin Prentiss Lucas Langham, a wealthy socialite widow from Houston, Texas, and mother of a teenage son and daughter.

The date was June 19, 1931.

The bridegroom was Clark Gable, just 30 years old.

It was not a widely-publicized wedding. Metro-Goldwyn-Mayer didn't want it to be. The studio's publicity hounds were terrified by the surprise marriage.

Why?

The box-office!

What would Gable's vast legions of female idolaters say, the studio wondered? How would those millions of women who dreamt of Gable as their lover, react when they found out that Clark had married a widow eleven years older than himself?

So the studio put the lid on the marriage. It succeeded—but not for long. News like this has a way of getting out and, despite all that was done to keep publicity down, the world soon knew that Gable had married a lovely Texas widow.

Who was Maria Rhea Franklin Prentiss Lucas Langham?

To the public, she was at once equated with the wealthy divorcee from Texas to whom Josephine Dillon had referred, without mentioning her name—the woman who "could do more for him financially."

Gable had met Rhea Langham, as she called herself for brevity's sake, back in 1927 when he had been in Houston with the touring stock company. Later, when he was on Broadway, Miss Langham came to New York and renewed her friendship with Clark. But there was nothing serious then in their relationship, because Gable was married to Josephine Dillon.

Then, after his divorce, Rhea came to Hollywood.

By that time Clark was a star. And if Rhea's bank account had anything to do with their falling in love, as Miss Dillon claimed, the facts fail to support her.

Gable didn't need money when he took Rhea for his second wife. He was making six hundred and fifty dollars a week, more than he had ever made in his life on a steady weekly basis. Only for one brief period of several weeks had he made more—seven hundred and fifty—when he worked on *Painted Desert*. In any case, that kind of money was far more than Gable had been accustomed to and more than he could ever require for his living needs. Clark was not a squanderer; he was a frugal man and his needs were never extravagant.

So, obviously, Clark didn't marry Rhea for her money.

But Rhea brought something else into Gable's life he had never known before—class.

Rhea was a society woman and, once married to Clark, she opened doors to places and people that the one-time farm boy could not have reached even with his fame and own high income alone. Rhea was Gable's key to the better things in life which he had never known.

She showed Clark the way to acquire social grace and poise, introduced him to her society friends, and sponsored him in one of the posh Los Angeles country clubs which, to a down-to-earth guy like Gable, held a strange new fascination in those years.

Moreover she got him into the Blue Book of Society— for whatever it meant.

And the studio moguls who had feared the consequences of Gable's marriage to his career, found, happily, that they had underestimated Gable's magnetism. His public accepted marriage to Rhea without deserting their idol, without losing one iota of interest in their hero. Marriage to Rhea lost Clark none of his vast popularity, which was still in the ascendancy.

Nor did marriage to Rhea slow down Gable's ever-increasing schedule of movie-making. In that year of 1931, the new heart throb of America's women was featured in leading or starring roles no less than a dozen times.

But suddenly marriage to Rhea seemed to change Gable. As if trying to discredit Josephine Dillon's contention that he was all-absorbed in his career and film work, Clark took his marriage seriously—and took Rhea's children to heart.

"His home life," as Rhea described it, "was that of a 'man's man' who was incidentally in the acting profession." More than a few times Clark emphasized to Rhea that he regarded pictures as a business, and talked about them as such—that is, when he did talk about them he did so no more than the average business man, who will tell his wife about new investments and discuss things with her.

"Clark read a great deal—scripts, of course," Rhea said. "But he also read magazines and books."

One night when Clark curled up in bed with a copy of *The Pickwick Papers*, Rhea turned to him and asked:

"Clark, you've read that old book at least a half dozen times. Why?"

"Funny you should ask," Clark said calmly. "I like it."

"He was that way about biographies and poetry—sometimes even detective stories," Rhea related. "But that old copy of *Pickwick Papers* was his favorite. He just read and reread it."

Clark scarcely ever went to bed without reading a little, no matter how late it was.

Along toward the third or fourth month of their marriage, Rhea was prompted one day when Clark was leaving for the golf course to ask why he was going. Gable turned to his wife and looked at her, puzzled.

"What do you mean?" he asked. "Do you object to my playing golf?"

"Of course not," Rhea said. "But why don't you show some interest in other sports?"

"That's a challenge," Gable replied. "I'll take you up on it."

And he did.

Before long Clark took up skeet shooting and he became an expert at it. His enthusiasm for the sport led him to join such notables of the day as John Barrymore, Gary Cooper, and Robert Montgomery in many pleasant afternoons on the range. Once Clark acquired the high degree of skill required, he entered skeet tournaments.

His greatest thrill came one day when he hit forty-nine out of fifty! A judge fell flat on his face running over to congratulate Clark.

"Mr. Gable," the thoroughly flustered judge said, after dusting himself off, "it *takes* me great pleasure in presenting you with this award."

It was Gable's proudest achievement—a gold medal.

When he returned home that afternoon, Rhea saw that Clark was radiant and aglow over something. She asked him what had happened.

"You are now married to a champion," Clark beamed proudly, pulling out the medal and exhibiting it to Rhea and the children.

"Now that you're such a good shot," Rhea put in, "you can take me hunting."

"How about some mountain lions?" Clark challenged, trying to frighten Rhea out of the idea.

"Suits me fine," Rhea replied. "When do we leave?"

Her answer almost floored Clark. But he went ahead and

made arrangements and in a few weeks they were off to Arizona hunting the critters. Later they went to Utah, and another time to Wyoming.

Rhea also interested Clark in other sports and activities—horseback riding and fishing.

Marriage to Rhea had given Clark a ready-made family. The children, Georgeanne, then 15, and Alfred Lucas, 10, were two easy-to-love youngsters and Clark at once fell in love with them. He played with them at home, he interested himself in their schoolwork and in their problems.

With the boy, Clark found increasing delight in trying to mold him into his idea of a man. He would take him on hikes, fishing, and swimming. That was at first. Later, Clark interested him in other things.

"This is a gun," Clark said one day when he felt Alfred was ready to learn about weapons. "You never point it at anyone unless you intend to kill that person—and that's something you will never want to do. But if you use it properly, for target shooting and for hunting, it will give you hours of happiness and pleasure as it has done for me."

The boy listened to his stepfather until he finished lecturing, then asked:

"Dad, tell me this—are you sure this is a gun and not a rifle?"

Clark looked at the boy expressionless for a moment. Then he burst into a roar of laughter. The kid had him—it was a rifle, but Clark had thought that, to simplify the explanation, he would, as many people do, refer to the weapon as a gun.

After that Clark took Alfred on a number of hunting trips.

But this happy portrait of family life was not destined to last. While there was little written in the newspapers and magazines about Gable and his family, the film colony became aware at a rather early date that the marriage was not fated to succeed. Rumblings of trouble began to roll through the movie capital even before Clark and Rhea had celebrated their first wedding anniversary on June 19, 1932.

No one was quite able to pinpoint the trouble, but it was there nevertheless. As it was to be learned later, when the truth and some of the facts became public, "misunderstandings" became the chief bone of contention between Clark and Rhea. With the studio demanding more and more of his time for bigger and better roles, Gable had less and less time to devote to Rhea and the children. Moreover, when he arrived home after a full day's work on the lot, Gable was bushed and, as Rhea put it, "difficult." Thus there was a basis for some misunderstanding, which was bound to come about.

But, beyond that, Rhea seemed to be confounded by one extremely embarrassing situation in her marriage to Gable with which she could not reconcile herself. It was created by Gable's first wife, Josephine Dillon, who was continuing to use her married name although the divorce had parted her and Clark for all time.

The first Mrs. Gable told newsmen—and that's how the story got out—that Mrs. Clark Gable No. 2 had phoned her on several occasions and demanded that Josephine resume her maiden name or, at least, drop her former husband's name. Miss Dillon said that Rhea even threatened legal action.

"I told her," Miss Dillon said, "that I would not drop the name. I said I would go right on using my married name.

"The quarrel occasionally ended with one or the other of us angrily hanging up the receiver. But it never made any difference to me—I was determined to keep the name. And I did."

While Rhea Langham and Clark Gable had their arguments and differences to cast unhappiness on their marriage, they also had their moments of contentment and deep satisfaction together.

Clark continued to devote himself almost completely to his stepson, who was also his mother's everlasting pride and joy. The youngster was thrilled going hunting and camping with his stepfather and grew to love Clark as his own father.

And despite the continuing dissension that began to cloud her marriage, Rhea, nevertheless, never ceased to work in her husband's best interests. Cultured, attractive, and a delightful hostess, Rhea came to be regarded by the film colony as Gable's perfect helpmeet. Her own background in handling her late first husband's business interests that had been willed to her was an essentially important factor that influenced her role in keeping Clark's business affairs and fast-changing fortunes on an orderly basis. She served as his chief adviser in business and studio matters and guided him through financial problems with a deft and steady hand.

# 7

## *The Gable Star Keeps Rising*

CLARK GABLE MOVED INEXO-
rably up, up, up to stardom, making picture after picture, roaring to the cinematic heights as the master of masculinity and conqueror of feminine hearts. He was a workhorse as he

toiled in *A Free Soul, Men in White, Red Dust, China Seas, Susan Lennox, Call of the Wild, Idiot's Delight, Strange Interlude, No Man of Her Own, The White Sister, Hold Your Man, Test Pilot, Hell Divers, Polly of the Circus,* and a host of others in those early years.

Gable's roster of leading ladies reads like a Who's Who of Moviedom. Besides Norma Shearer and Joan Crawford there were Greta Garbo, Jean Harlow, Carole Lombard, Helen Hayes, Loretta Young, Myrna Loy, Rosalind Russell, and many others.

Through these films, as the Gable fame mounted and the box-office receipts leap-frogged to unprecedented figures, Clark persisted in keeping a level head about himself. He insisted that he was not an actor—that he was just himself. In his dressing rooms he always hung up signs and reminders of the days when he was a struggling actor and a lumber worker in Oregon. Across the mementos he wrote such legends as, "Just to remind you, Gable."

There were many, many fascinating aspects about Gable that enabled him to climb to the rarefied heights which no man before him—or since—has reached in Hollywood, but perhaps the one peculiarity of his overwhelming popularity was the attitude of the millions of women who adored him. While most other leading men aroused the fair sex with desires to "mother" them, Gable evoked a uniquely different feeling. When women watched him on the screen they did not want to mother Clark Gable. They wanted to make love to him!

When Gable would look at his leading lady, with his forehead furrowed and his right eyebrow cocked quizzically, it would bring the women to the edge of their seats. They would wait there breathlesssly for the thrilling moment that had to follow when Gable would command, "Come here, baby!"

Oh, what that line did to women!

And the men loved it, too.

The Gable popularity indicator kept rising.

From his very first performance, Clark Gable indicated to the movie critics and audiences alike that he was heading places. His performance in *Painted Desert,* which went by without landing him a contract—although it attracted the attention of Minna Wallis, who got him signed by MGM eventually—was a rather unimpressive vehicle which did not draw critical acclaim for Clark.

Nor did he attract rave notices for his first major MGM film, *A Free Soul,* which brought him together with Norma Shearer. His acting was considered routine in this vehicle—although the slap that shook up Miss Shearer made up for all the acting polish Gable may have lacked at the time. The audiences raved over Clark, who played a gangster. The acting honors were stolen in this film by Lionel Barrymore, who played Stephen Ashe, a hard-drinking lawyer who defends Clark and gets him cleared.

In reviewing the film, Mordaunt Hall, the former New York *Times* critic, concluded that "Talking pictures are by no means elevated by the presentation of *A Free Soul,*" which premiered at the Astor Theatre. Hall found Barrymore's performance was the only believable one, while Miss Shearer was "called upon to act a part which is quite unsuited to her intelligent type of beauty." Going on, Hall said, "Clark Gable is all very well as a gangster, but it is problematical whether a young woman of Miss Shearer's type would ever become enamored of an individual who behaves as he does here."

Well, whether or not Miss Shearer's type could become enamored was answered by the women all over America—and their answer was that they could be enamored of Clark Gable. Head over heels.

Mordaunt Hall also was a bit critical of Gable's performance in *Men in White,* in which he co-starred with Myrna Loy —but the critic paid high tribute to the new phenomenon of the screen when he wrote, "Mr. Gable dominates his scenes, not, however, as a surgeon, but as a *romantic individual.* And even then he is always Mr. Gable and not Dr. George Ferguson." There it was—the Gable image taking hold of the silver screen, becoming an individual who could not be mistaken for anyone else but Clark Gable. The trademark was set.

Gable hit it big in *Dancing Lady,* his first musical, which cast him with glamorous Joan Crawford, a disciple of Terpsichore from the realms of burlesque. As Janie, she falls afoul of the law, only to be rescued from the bastille by Newton, a personable playboy in the person of Franchot Tone. Tone is the backer of a big show, and through his influence gruff director Patch, played by Gable, is prevailed upon to make room in the cast for a gal of Miss Crawford's hidden talents. The plot thickens when Joan makes good and asks Tone to live up to his promise—to let her be if she and the show succeed. Tone pulls his dough out and that sends Gable to the bottle, disgustedly, and the opening curtain is uncertain. But Joan gets wind of the scheme, comes back to the show, it opens, and is a smash. And Clark gets his reward—Joan.

*China Seas* was another vehicle that gave Clark added stature in the eyes of moviegoers. This was his second time around with Jean Harlow, with whom he had previously starred in *Red Dust.* But the raves over his performance in *Dust* were a whisper compared with those for *China Seas.* This was a mighty melodrama with every element of entertainment—it was tumultuous romance, rip-roaring action, exciting background, and it had a genuine all-star cast. Gable had top billing, followed by Jean Harlow, Wallace Beery,

Lewis Stone, Rosalind Russell, Dudley Digges, and C. Aubrey Smith. The *New York Mirror's* Bland Johaneson cheered the picture in these words:

"*China Seas* is a powerful melodrama, lively and punchy enough to thrill the most exacting fan. It's a smash picture with a smash cast. Don't miss it."

And the hits kept coming. Gable was the hottest property of any movie company in the film capital. His star kept climbing.

When he was paired with Greta Garbo, the greatest and most fascinating star of her day, it was a mighty compliment to Gable. And his performance with this magnificent woman of mystery, in *Susan Lennox,* solidified his hold on the realm of stardom beyond any doubt; Gable established forever his ability to express the pathos, the longing, the searing sorrow of the drama which he had been consigned to play. Both Garbo and Gable dimmed the memories of past triumphs with this one—and when Gable took Garbo in his arms, it epitomized all the romance that had ever scorched the silver screen in years past. There was nothing like it.

Then came *Test Pilot* and another great screen heroine leaped into Clark Gable's arms to make them a sizzling duo in a love story of a beautiful romance that narrowly misses a tragic ending by a twist of fate. Miss Loy plays Ann, the test pilot's wife. Gable is the pilot, Jim, irrepressible in his job, the most thrilling and most dangerous in the field of flying.

The picture also saw Spencer Tracy in one of several films in which he co-starred with Clark Gable, playing Damon to Clark's Pythias, and turning in a triumphant performance as always. Lionel Barrymore, Samuel S. Hinds, Marjorie Main, and Virginia Grey were among the others in starring roles.

Kate Cameron, the *New York Daily News* critic, gave *Test Pilot* the newspaper's top rating, four stars, and had this to say:

"Metro-Goldwyn-Mayer is presenting today at the Capitol Theatre the most beautiful and thrilling aviation picture it, or any other studio, has ever produced . . ." She cheered Miss Loy and said the Garbos, Bette Davises, Katharine Hepburns, and Luise Rainers could make room for Miss Loy to sit with them in their places of honor as great actresses. As for Gable, Miss Cameron had only the highest praise.

Gable continued to draw accolades.

*Idiot's Delight,* which followed, starred Clark as a song-and-dance man in a striped suit and Norma Shearer as a phony Russian refugee in a slinky gown, balancing a long cigaret holder. The film, whose theme exposes the pointlessness of militarism, portrays Gable as Harry Van, a breezy, hard-headed knockabout hoofer, and Miss Shearer, as Irene, a shabby little vaudevillian with a knack for being the most atrociously amusing liar. The entire film, start to finish, is smooth, fast-moving, and boisterously farcical—and Gable and Shearer shared full honors for this achievement.

Rose Pelswick's review in the *Journal-American* raved about *Idiot's Delight* and called it "a hugely amusing show, a robust and smartly spun-out comedy in which Norma Shearer and Clark Gable check in performances that are nothing short of hilarious."

That's the way it went for Gable—up, up, up. Better roles. More acclaim. Cheers from the critics. And bigger and still bigger lines at the box-office. Gable was the greatest.

Before we get too far ahead in our story, let us return to a day in 1934, while *Dancing Lady* was in production. Even then, Clark had had three dozen pictures under his belt. And suddenly, he felt the strain of his furiously-paced movie career beginning to tell on his health.

Pulling guns on people, slapping women in the face, and running through the hectic action scenes of movie after movie had worn Gable down to a frazzle. He had lost considerable weight. During several visits to his doctor, Clark was told that he might regain some of his strength and stamina if he would yield to a couple of operations. He had been bothered by chronic colds, which were brought on by his tonsils—and the doctor said they had to come out. Gable also had been bedeviled by occasional attacks of pain on his right side. The doctor had the solution for that, too—take the appendix out.

Just about this time, Metro put him in *Dancing Lady*. Gable was disgusted with the way the picture was going but his health had him in even more desperate straits. When the picture was over Gable was told they wanted to remake some scenes. He balked. He told MGM in very blunt language, "My health isn't what it used to be. It's pretty bad, in fact. This part you gave me is pretty bad, too. But bad as the part is, it isn't as bad as my health. So, I'm going to follow my doctor's advice and have a few operations. That'll take care of my health as well as my part in *Dancing Lady*, too."

And Gable was off to the hospital.

Tonsils were yanked first, then after a brief period of recovery, the appendix went.

Altogether Gable was confined to the hospital nearly nine weeks. At the end of the period, he returned home to Rhea and convalesced several days before finally showing up at the studio.

Gable was greeted at Metro with surprising coldness.

"They thought," he explained later, "that I had taken evasive action to avoid *Dancing Lady*. They just couldn't understand that my health had reached the danger point and that I had to begin taking care of it."

A Metro executive, Eddie Mannix, told Clark:

"We've decided to send you over to Columbia Pictures on a loanout." This meant Gable was being loaned to another studio—and it was a slap in the face.

Gable was astonished.

"I was so sore," Gable said, "that I turned on my heels and walked out, slamming the door as though I was trying to jam it through the frame. At that time Columbia was on the wrong side of the tracks in the motion picture business, and being sent there was a this-will-teach-you-a-lesson deal. I didn't know anybody at Columbia, but I'd gotten a call in a couple of days from the studio and was told, 'Report to Frank Capra.' So I reported to him.

"Before I went into his office—I was still sore—I belted down a couple of fast drinks. Then I marched in to see Capra. He could see I wasn't happy, and he sat there with the script in his hand trying to be tactful. Frank is a gentle guy.

" 'Sit down, Clark,' he said, drawing up a chair, 'I want to tell you about our story.'

"I was still hopping mad. I jerked the script out of his hand and said, 'I don't want to talk to you about it. Just let me take the script home. I'll read it. Then I'll talk to you.'

"Frank, being such a nice guy, was tolerant of my attitude, which, to put it mildly, wasn't good. He didn't know I felt that I had just been swept out of MGM's executive offices with the morning trash. I took the script home and read it. I had a couple of more drinks and I wondered about the script.

" 'It couldn't be *that* good,' I told myself. 'I'd better read it again.'

"So I had dinner and read it again. It was still good. The next morning I called Frank and said, 'I want to apologize for my behavior yesterday. I was rude and I had no reason to be. You've got a fine script. Why you've chosen me to be in it I don't know. You've never seen me play comedy on the screen. But if you think I can do it, I'll try. But after three or four days, if you don't like what you see on the screen, you can call the whole thing off and there'll be no hard feelings.' "

Capra agreed.

The next day Clark Gable showed up at Columbia to begin work.

It was then he met his co-star, Claudette Colbert.

The film was *It Happened One Night*.

# 8

## Long Live the King!

CLARK GABLE, BIG AS HE WAS
in films in 1934, still wasn't so big to director Frank Capra as
to command an invitation to the projection room to watch the
daily rushes of *It Happened One Night*. But every day, after
he saw the action on the small studio screen, Capra came out
with a smile on his face that told Gable the picture would not
be called off. It was going well.

Gable had had experience in comedy before, but not in
films. His last stage performance had been in a satirical comedy, *Love, Honor and Betray*, which starred Alice Brady on
Broadway. But almost everyone by then had forgotten that
Clark Gable had a New York stage background.

"I couldn't blame them for forgetting," Gable said. "I
didn't exactly set the town on fire, and I was brought into the
motion picture business as a heavy because of my performance as Killer Mears in *The Last Mile*. But I knew what I had
to do when I read the script of *It Happened One Night*. I
knew I had to play it cool and relaxed. And that's exactly how
I went about it."

*It Happened One Night* opens with Gable, playing a New
York newspaper reporter named Peter, phoning his boss and
telling him what he thinks of him. Peter is promptly fired.

He gets on a Miami-to-New York bus and there meets Ellen,
played by Claudette Colbert, a headstrong young heiress who
has just married a fortune hunter in New York. Her father,
who objected to the marriage, had taken her off on his yacht right
after the ceremony and locked her in a cabin until she
would consent to have the marriage annulled. But Ellen, determined to have her own way, busted out, jumped overboard,
swam to shore, and boarded the bus.

Ellen's father sends detectives to sniff his daughter's trail,
but she manages to elude them. Peter recognizes the runaway
heiress from her pictures and the big black newspaper headlines that clarion a nationwide search for the heiress. There's
a $10,000 reward for anyone who turns her in to papa.

Peter and Ellen start off fighting and in nothing flat each
has formed an opinion of the other. Peter regards Ellen as a
spoiled brat who means only one thing to him—a big story
that will get him back his job. But then there is a big storm

and the bus bogs down at an auto camp. When one of the passengers recognizes Ellen, she and Peter leave the bus and hitch-hike to another auto camp.

Sparkling situation follows sparkling situation as the story takes some delightfully adroit turns.

Peter and Ellen end up for the night in the same room at the auto camp; he rigs up a blanket that he calls the "Walls of Jericho" to separate their single beds. There follow many amusing incidents, not the least of which are a scene in which Peter shows Ellen how to dunk doughnuts in coffee; another in which he shows her how to stop a car with feminine guile while hitch-hiking, and a sequence back on the bus again when Peter pretends to be a gunman in order to scare off a passenger who threatened to expose Ellen and get the reward offered by her father.

Gable was superb. His lines were witty, pithy, and punchy; he put them over with remarkable smoothness that lent a new dimension to the Gable who had until then been known as a "heavy." He showed a tremendous flair for comedy. Miss Colbert herself was magnificent.

Critics unanimously acclaimed *It Happened One Night* as a hit—and the vast majority agreed it was the best picture of 1934.

The film opened in New York's Radio City Music Hall on George Washington's Birthday, February 22. One of the rave reviewers was the New York *Journal-American's* Rose Pelswick, who said:

"It's only February, but even by the time that December rolls around, *It Happened One Night* will still be one of the best pictures of the year . . . Its stars are Clark Gable, in what is easily his best role to date, and Claudette Colbert, who is elegant, too . . . Gable is the big surprise of the piece. He's played romantic heroes before this, and he's played tough guys. But here, in addition to being romantic and two-fisted, he displays a gorgeous flair for comedy. And, given a script and dialogue studded with laughs and brilliant direction, he turns in a performance that's something to tell the neighbors about . . . Gable is simply grand."

This was the finest review that any Gable picture had ever received. The critics, to a man, were convinced that Gable now was not only a popular star—but an actor of considerable talent.

As the picture made its rounds of the nation's theatres, record breaking crowds turned out everywhere to view the sensational Gable-Colbert acting team, and many stories circulated about how both had practically turned their noses up at the parts when they were offered, neither giving a second thought to the chance that the picture would be a hit. Legends were created about the classic scenes in the film—like the piggybank scene, the bus sequence in which the passengers sing "The Daring Young Man on the Flying Trapeze," and the part in which Miss Colbert lifts her skirt while thumbing a ride and causes a passing motorist to slam on his brakes. The stories went that all these scenes were thought up on the spur of the moment by director Capra as he went along.

Actually they were not shot off the cuff but carefully plotted into the script by Capra and Bob Riskin, who was the writer. In fact, it was scenes like those that brought Gable back to Capra, after he had read the script, feeling like a heel for having been rude to him at their initial meeting.

And it was scenes like those that ultimately brought about the following dispatch in early 1935 from the film city:

HOLLYWOOD, Feb. 27 (AP).—Claudette Colbert and Clark Gable were voted to have given the best screen performances in 1934 by the Academy of Motion Pictures Arts and Sciences at its seventh annual banquet here tonight.

The awards given to Miss Colbert and Gable were for their appearance in the picture It Happened One Night, in which they co-starred.

The banquet was a colorful affair, attended by the flower of the film colony. More than 800 persons heard Irvin S. Cobb, author and humorist and a recent recruit to screen ranks as a comedian, praise the winners as he presented the awards.

And there it was—an Academy Award for Clark Gable! Indeed, now he had reached the cinematic heavens; the dream of that tall, gawky, dark-faced boy of sixteen who sat in the top gallery of a small Akron theatre looking down on the stage of performers in The Bird of Paradise, had come true at last. That scene, back in 1917, never would have suggested that the boy in the balcony seat would be the man who would be worshipped by women all over the world, admired by its men—and hailed as an Academy Award winner.

But Gable did it. He did it with his determination and drive, his devotion and durability, and his will and willingness and wistfulness and wonder-working ways.

At this time, Clark was in the midst of the busiest and most important movie-making schedule of his career. Metro had bought one of the strongest and most dramatic sea stories ever written—the fateful voyage of H.M.S. Bounty, which sailed out of Portsmouth, England, in 1778, never to return to the home port. The weird and exciting history of the Bounty formed the basis of a novel by Charles Nordhoff and James Hall. As early as 1933, Metro had bought the rights from director Frank Lloyd, who had taken an option on the book for $12,500. When the deal went through, Lloyd was signed to direct the film.

By 1935 everything, after two years of preliminaries, was ready. For its cast, MGM could not overlook any longer the star who was their number one box-office attraction—Clark Gable. So the starring roles were announced:

Clark would portray Fletcher Christian; Charles Laughton would be the tyrannical Captain Bligh; Franchot Tone would get the part of young Roger Byam.

For a year previously, director Lloyd had made excursions to the South Seas, to Pitcairn Island, to get authentic background atmosphere shots for the adventure yarn. Pitcairn was populated by descendants of the escaped mutineers from the *Bounty*. Lloyd and his staff of 51 technicians and more than 100 tons of equipment returned with 80,000 feet of atmosphere film. Then came the announcement that the film would go in production.

A replica of the *Bounty* was built from plans of the original ship supplied by the British Admiralty, and two modern barges, towed by tugs, transported the equipment and props to Catalina Island. To house the troupe, MGM leased the entire isthmus tent city and many resort buildings, including Banning House. Speedboats skimmed back and forth between the isthmus and the Hollywood mainland, and from Avalon, fifty minutes away, with the daily rushes and special messages. And the good ship *Betty-O* daily brought food from Avalon to feed the cast. High-speed vessels also were put in service to transport the players from the isthmus to the *Bounty* which sailed full-rigged from ten to twenty miles off the island.

Labor crews also built roads to inaccessible areas—one road over steep cliffs was three miles long and led to "Matavai Bay" where South Sea natives appeared in scenes with the *Bounty* in the Pacific Ocean background. Another road, eight miles long, was carved on the windward side of the island to shoot a scene of a sailing vessel that was driven onto a reef to lend realism to the plot.

All in all, it was one of Hollywood's most spectacular and most authentic filmings to date.

After the picture was completed, a nationwide campaign to publicize the film was launched. Then came its opening in New York's Capitol Theatre. The critics gave it a tremendous reception. While one or two critics found fault with the length of the film—two hours and fifteen minutes—there was no doubt about Laughton's performance, nor of Gable's, nor Tone's. It was unanimously agreed that their acting was superb.

Laughton himself came away with a performance that would forever be his trademark in the eyes of the film-going public; comedians and mimics by the hundreds would emulate the paunchy, cruel Captain Bligh on stage and radio and later, in time to come, on television. As for Gable, his acting once more indicated to the critics as well as to his still-growing legion of fans that he was an actor of the first order. His portrayal of Fletcher Christian, as first mate, a hard but humane task master, rebellious against the captain's cruelty, established Gable's star in the firmament of acting greats more solidly than ever.

His popularity soared still higher.

Late that year of 1935, Clark went off by himself on a six-week vacation trip through Mexico, Central and South America. It was really a combination triumphal tour and hare-and-hound chase, for Gable found the Latin American señoritas quite a formidable bunch.

Returning one early November morning from his tour, Gable descended the gangplank from the Munson liner *Pan America*, which docked at the foot of Brooklyn's Montague Street, looking like a man who had wafted through a hurricane—a hurricane of women.

Dressed with smart carelessness in a light flannel suit with dark stripes, an olive drab shirt, a soft crumpled fedora, and smoking a bulldog pipe, Gable reported on his vacation trip which had taken him by plane, via Mexico City and the Canal Zone, to the West Coast of South America, across the Andes to Rio, then by ship on the return.

At Santiago, a crowd of Chilenos, mostly women, had chased Gable and an American friend, Harry Moscowitz, into the latter's hotel suite, broke down the door, appropriated Moscowitz' hair brushes, pajamas, tooth brushes, and other items of personal belongings—in the belief that they were Clark's. The frenzied females also smashed furniture and, lovingly, roughed up Gable.

"It was awful . . . like a hurricane had hit the room," Gable recalled.

"In Valparaiso, three gendarmes who came to my help when I took refuge from a press of exuberant women promptly pulled out autograph books instead of trying to restrain the fans."

"You know something," he added as an afterthought, "women are crazy, I guess . . ."

Gable had returned just in time to be on hand for the opening of *Mutiny on the Bounty* the next day at the Capitol.

At the premiere, New York City's Finest, nearly one hundred strong, exerted every muscle in their bodies to keep back the surging, screaming throngs of women who descended on Broadway to get a glimpse of their idol in the flesh. Gable was hurried through the crowd under a fifteen-man police escort which had its hands and faces scratched and bloodied trying to protect the handsome screen hero from the enthusiastic onslaught of the fans.

When it was time to leave, the manager of the Capitol suggested to Clark that he sneak out a side entrance which would take him away from the maddening throng of humanity that still lingered outside the theatre nearly two and a half hours later.

"Nothing doing," Clark remarked. "They came here to see me and I'm going out there. The day they stop coming around is the day when I'm going to be through in this business. I owe them the decency of making an appearance. They deserve it. I'm going out there."

Clark walked out into the crowd. As police held the mob in check, Clark walked to a waiting studio limousine, waving and smiling. He was driven away to the Waldorf-Astoria Hotel—with women and girls chasing the car for several blocks along the route, until, panting, breathless, they could no longer keep up.

He was lucky to get out of New York with his clothes and belongings. He barely made it to the station, a mere step ahead of a charging horde of women. What was it he'd said about South American señoritas being rough . . . ?

When Gable left New York for Hollywood, he was going back with the problems of his marriage to Rhea virtually settled. The newspapers by then had already made the announcement with headlines like these:

### Clark Gable Parting from Wife

And there it was—Clark Gable's second marriage was on the rocks.

Immediately ten million feminine hearts began to pound. Immediately ten million—give or take a dozen—proposals of marriage poured in from Boston and Baltimore, Peoria and Peru, St. Louis and St. Joseph, Seattle and Sacramento. From everywhere, Clark's adoring female fans wrote and pleaded to marry him.

Clark smiled. Metro smiled.

There was no question about it—Clark Gable was truly the lover and landlord of Hollywood—and of America.

He was the King—as yet uncrowned, but nevertheless the King!

# 9

## *Woman Troubles*

NOW THAT CLARK GABLE WAS
separated from his wife and talk of divorce was a daily ritual for the gossip columnists, the next logical step for Hollywood rumor makers was to forge a romantic link between the screen's handsome hero and every girl who was seen in his company. More often than not the target of shrewd publicity seekers anxious to hitch their wagons to his star, Gable became the victim of countless lies.

In whispers sometimes, printed items at other times, Clark was tied up with every lovely who so much as spoke with him. One day it would be Park Avenue society girl and fashion model Mary Taylor, another time the English actress Elizabeth Allen, who was married; and there were times when the columnists insisted Gable was romantically interested in Loretta Young. And so it went.

Another entry in the Gable marital guessing game was a blonde fireball with an infectious smile, dreamy bedroom eyes, an aura of mystery that was being compared by then to Garbo's and Dietrich's, a sultry voice that melted men's hearts. She was Carole Lombard, who was being seen in Clark's company perhaps more often than any of the others.

Who was Carole Lombard?

At the time, in early 1936, Carole Lombard was just another of the many dozens of potentially great screen actresses who seemed to have all the necessary qualities and talent credentials to hit greatness, but lacked merely the "stretch drive" to take them into the winner's circle.

Clark and Carole had known each other for something like four years at the time. They had co-starred in 1932 in *No Man of Her Own*, but they were not interested in each other then. Clark was married to Rhea and Carole was married to actor William Powell.

But in 1936, things had changed. Clark and Rhea were separated, although not divorced. Carole already was divorced from Powell. While legally still bound to a wife, Gable nevertheless floated from woman to woman—until Carole came along. Then something happened. The other women somehow all dropped out of his life and Carole became the central character, the feminine lead, on Clark Gable's romantic stage.

It all began at a party, the Mayfair Ball, in Hollywood. Carole had been escorted by a rising young Latin lover named Cesar Romero. Clark came alone. Somehow, Carole and Clark were drawn together and they talked and joked. Clark was immediately struck by Carole's zaniness and her memorable language, which was on the salty side. He thought about asking to take her home—although it bothered Clark that Cesar Romero might consider it an affront. But before the evening was over, Clark didn't have to worry about hurting Cesar's feelings. That was obviated by a sudden and unexpected development.

Gable and Lombard had their first fight!

"What did you mean by telling that reporter that I don't take myself seriously?" Carole demanded of Clark. "Who do you think you are—my critic?"

Carole was referring to a columnist's report that Clark had said he considered Carole a potentially great actress, that she was the only American-born actress who could really exude "glamor" on the screen, but didn't know how to make the most of it. And if she did make it as a glamor girl of the screen, it would be in spite of herself.

Clark tried to explain to Carole that he was only offering his comments in a constructive vein.

"I was simply trying to put the point across that you don't take yourself seriously," Gable told the fuming Carole. "I think you have a great capacity as an actress, both for mystery and glamor—and when I see you on the screen I get a sense of drama just by watching you flick your eyelashes."

Carole's eyes narrowed—and she started flicking her eyelashes mockingly at Clark. He began to sense her annoyance at what he was telling her, but Clark was not a quitter. He had made up his mind to tell Carole what he started out to put across.

"You're not a comedienne, although you're good at that, too. You are really a dramatic actress, and I'm willing to bet the world is going to hear about you and be aware of your talents some day."

Gable was getting into deeper trouble with every sentence —and Carole's patience was wearing wafer thin.

"With the right roles," Clark went on, "and, of course, you gotta have the right attitude, too, I think you might make it . . ."

Clark never finished the sentence. Carole leaped at him in utter impatience and scorn, shouting just one word—

"Nuts!"

Then Carole, her face flushed with anger, whirled around and stalked off to the other side of the ballroom.

Clark was left standing by himself. His face was red. But not from embarrassment. He was doing his damnedest to keep from laughing.

Needless to say, Carole left the party with Cesar. And Clark went home the way he had come—alone.

At the time, Carole had her own home in Brentwood, while Clark was living in his bachelor quarters in the Beverly-Wilshire Hotel.

The next morning, Clark was awakened by a loud and furry cooing. Still half asleep, he got out of bed to investigate and found a deliveryman had brought a huge cage. Inside it was a flock of seven white doves!

Carole had sent them—the doves of peace!

In time, the doves would become Carole's classic peace offering after every quarrel she'd have with Clark.

From that morning on, the dove trade in Hollywood and surrounding areas did a thriving business. For whenever a single harsh word was spoken by Carole to Clark, or vice-versa, then zoom—the dove would be flown in, an olive-branch clenched between its "teeth."

Clark also participated in Carole's zany antics, but he had his own bag of tricks to get back at her. One time a fan had sent Gable a 300-pound statue of himself as Christian in *Mutiny on the Bounty*. Some time later, Clark and Carole had another tiff.

One bright morning Carole opened the door to find 300 pounds of stone Gable on her front lawn, a garland of forget-me-nots twined around its throat, a red rose behind each ear.

"Why, that egotistical, big-headed, big-eared baboon," screamed Carole, and dashed for the phone. She burned up the wires for a half hour until she reached the party she was calling.

"Yes, yes, that's what I'm trying to tell you," Carole yelled into the phone. "Now get over here right now—right now!"

An hour later five men and a truck pulled up in front of the Lombard residence.

"That's it," Carole told the men, pointing to the statue. "You know what to do."

They did. Following Carole's orders they hauled it to the city dump.

As Clark continued to court Carole at the expense of the many other girls around Hollywood who had flocked to Gable's side after his separation from Rhea, it became apparent to everyone that wedding bells would ring out some day for the couple. But no one could say when. Clark himself insisted he was not prepared for a third marriage—not legally, not mentally.

But he did put himself on record about the kind of girl his next wife would be—he had her image well-crystallized in his mind:

"Looks and age don't cut any ice with me," he said. "They're not important. I've always sort of leaned toward the medium in height and size. However, if the right girl happens to be short and round or tall and thin, I suppose I'll think she's perfect. I've never believed in that bunk about a man's one ideal girl. I've had probably a dozen ideal girls in my life, each one being the person I happened to be in love with at the time.

"But I certainly don't like ultra-spectacular women, the ones who go in for startling make-up and clothes. I like the girls who look conservatively smart, with a smooth finish. No straggling hair or run-over heels or missing buttons. I never can remember any definite detail about a woman's clothes, but I always notice whether she matches in color schemes, whether she's put together right.

"But personality," Clark went on as he described what his next wife would be like, "would be a thousand times, ten thousand times more important to me. First of all, I admire girls with a sense of humor and with understanding, but not the fake kinds which you find so often. Girls don't have to open their eyes wide and hang breathlessly on a man's words to prove that they're interested and admiring. I like the kind of girl who has a grasp of masculine feelings. The girl who, when a man comes home tired on Friday night and says, 'Listen, honey, I don't feel up to going to the Jones' shindig. Let's grab a few old clothes and dig out for the weekend,' will say, 'It's okay with me.' And mean it.

"I always look twice at girls who are alive, vital, alert, on their toes. The weeping willow type, the languidly drooping ladies, never did appeal to me. The first woman I ever really fell for—I was about twenty at the time and she was around forty-five—was one of the most vivid, energetic women I've ever known. We were in the same theatrical company, touring the sticks. There was a young girl in the outfit, a beautiful kid, as I remember, but so languid and kittenish that I wanted to choke her.

"But it's ridiculous for me to be talking about the kind of girl I may marry some day. I'm not free to think of marrying anyone. And I'm not interested in romance and marriage at the present time.

"To tell you the truth, women scare me . . ."

There was little wonder that Gable was afraid of women. He had had his clothes almost torn off by eager, clawing feminine hands in every city of the United States, Mexico, and South America which he had visited; he had two unsuccessful marriages. Gable, indeed, may have been truly afraid of women.

But the women did not fear Gable. The women were wild over their film idol; so much so that by the time the official box-office figures for 1936 were in, Clark Gable officially became the screen's most popular star. In the annual national poll conducted by the film trade magazine *Boxoffice*, Gable was listed at the top of the list, displacing Shirley Temple, the dimpled darling, who finished second. Fred Astaire and Ginger Rogers were third that year, Robert Taylor fourth, and William Powell fifth.

Gable had ascended the loftiest plane of stardom. He was now the "King"—and the title was conferred on him in a manner that is still in some dispute. The most popular version is that Spencer Tracy, at a dinner marking Clark's ascendancy as top draw at the boxoffice, stood up at the dais and placed a cardboard crown on Gable's head, saying, "I crown thee 'King of Hollywood.' "

This, then, was Gable—the biggest attraction in Hollywood, or the world. And by far more famous and fancied than any king of royal blood who ruled the world.

But even kings sometimes will find their thrones may get a jolt during periods of unrest while they reign over their subjects. For Gable, the time of uncertainty descended like a thunderbolt from above one late January day of 1937 when headlines burst across the country with the obvious makings of a scandal.

### Mother of 4 Tells Gable to Confess

It was a headline sparked by a forty-seven-year-old Englishwoman, Mrs. Violet Wells Norton, who claimed Clark Gable was the father of her thirteen-year-old daughter, Gwendoline.

Gable categorically denied paternity of the girl, but he was forced to stand in the dock and fight the charge in the open with every bit of strength and resource at his command. It was a challenge that Gable had never before encountered. But he was up to it.

The story begins with a letter. It was a letter sent by Mrs. Norton to Clark from Winnipeg, Canada, on March 30, 1936. In it she reproaches the screen idol for not sending for her and "our daughter Gwendoline" and financing the child's start in movies as an actress.

One of the letters Mrs. Norton wrote to Clark, whom she addressed as "Frank," read like this:

Frank Dear.

It's Leap Year so I can tell you I still love you . . . I have loved you all these years and since I have seen you on the screen at work how I have longed to talk to you.

You are free and so am I. Why not renew our friendship? Nobody need know. Let's go away together.

I am a different woman to when you knew me. I am full of pep and romance. I don't have my hands filled with children.

Mrs. Norton claimed that Clark and she had carried on a romance in England, some fifteen years before. That, roughly, would have been 1922, while Gable was toiling with a road show on the Oregon Trail.

Clark did nothing about the initial letters. He didn't even bother to reply and, perhaps, advise the woman she was laboring under a delusion if she thought he was her long-lost boyfriend.

But then Mrs. Norton sent similar letters to columnists around the country, including Walter Winchell. Winchell called Gable and asked, "What gives with this broad?"

"I don't know her from Suzy Sooks in Saskatchewan," Gable told Winchell. "She's trying to blackmail me."

"Don't you know what to do?" Winchell asked.

"What?"

"Go to the authorities," Winchell advised. "This is blackmail and this dame is using the mails to defraud. You can have her arrested. And jailed."

"And what about the publicity?" Gable asked.

"If you're in the clear—and I'm sure you are—you'll be more popular after this is over than ever, if it's possible to be more popular."

"Thanks for the advice, Walter," Gable said. "I'm going to report it."

Gable went to the United States District Attorney in Los Angeles, a branch of the U. S. Attorney's office in Washington, and revealed the sordid story of attempted blackmail. He brought the letters as evidence.

The government prosecutor, John Powell, then questioned Gable about the facts. Powell had to know two important things—did Gable remember where he was in 1922, 1923, and 1924 during the time of the purported romance, and, more importantly, could he prove it?

"My answer is yes to both questions," Clark answered. "I was in Oregon in 1922 and 1923, in California in 1924. I can prove it. I have my pay stubs from the lumber camp at home and probably can get a half dozen witnesses who could testify for me—including an old girlfriend I had up there while I worked as an actor. And, of course, there's my first wife whom I met in Oregon."

"Good enough for me," prosecutor Powell said. "We'll swear out a warrant for Mrs. Norton's arrest."

And Mrs. Norton, who had come from England, by way of Canada, to Hollywood to hound Clark, was arrested. A speedy indictment on the evidence followed. Then came the trial in Los Angeles' Federal Court. Accused along with Mrs. Norton was a private eye named Jack L. Smith, who had financed her trip to Hollywood and had sought, independent of his client's efforts, to pursuade Metro to set up a $50,000 trust fund for Gwendoline to "avoid the dirty publicity that will come out of this mess."

Clark's first day in court was like a Roman holiday. Hundreds of women mobbed the courthouse and besieged Gable as he walked in, almost tearing the clothes from his back. Barred from the already overflowing courtroom, the women poured out into the halls and when they spotted him as he came toward them, they rushed headlong at Clark. They pulled his necktie, stole his lapel handkerchief, and were clawing at his coat in the scuffle. Only the quick intercession of courtroom guards saved Gable from his adoring fans. The disturbance was so uproarious that Judge George Cosgrave was impelled to rap loudly for order.

After straightening his attire, Gable made a calm entrance into the courtroom as the first witness against Mrs. Norton.

Mrs. Norton made quite a contrast to other women who had figured in the life of the handsome screen lover, the Number One heart throb of American womanhood. Mrs. Norton, leaping into life now, was a dowdy creature who wore a set of artificial teeth which chattered like castanets when she became excited. She became excited when she was told Clark Gable had never been in England, where she claimed the "romance" between herself and Gable took place late in 1922, and continued thereafter following the birth of her child.

"So 'e said that, did 'e?" she growled, her double chin trembling with indignation. "Well, 'e's an arrant fraud. 'E's Frank Billings, that's 'oo 'e is! I could tell from the w'y 'e mykes love to Joan Crawford."

Conceding she was the mother of four illegitimate children, Mrs. Norton rolled her eyes expressively as she recounted her asserted pecadillos with "Billings."

"We was livin' side by side in Bellericay, Essex, England, in 1922," she explained. "I wasn't married to me 'usband, you see, an' there was a lot of rowin' atween us. So one day Billings, or Gybles, as 'e calls 'isself now, 'eard us, an' 'e sez, 'Violet,' 'e sez, 'I have been lovin' you right along.'

"I was a looker then, I was, but ten years older than 'im, so I tell 'im to go along. 'E grabs me wrist and turns the key in the door, an' there he was. An' it wasn't the only time, either."

When Gable took the stand, his testimony was short and to the point.

Q. Were you ever in England?
A. No.
Q. Were you ever known as Frank Billings?
A. No.
Q. Do you know Mrs. Norton?

A. No.
Q. Are you the father of her daughter, Gwendoline?
A. No.

Hollywood radio commentator Jimmy Fidler took the stand to tell of receiving a letter, in which Mrs. Norton offered to sell the story of her "love affair with Clark Gable."

The trial took a sensational turn when the prosecution called titian-haired, shapely Franz Doerfler, a struggling actress, to the stand. She had been Gable's girlfriend up in Oregon, before he'd met his first wife. As she was told the charge by Mrs. Norton—that Gable had fathered her child in England—Miss Doerfler, her eyes flashing with determination, broke out with:

"That is perfectly ridiculous. Clark and I were playing in a small stock company together at Astoria, Oregon, at the time." Miss Doerfler went on to say that their dates came to an abrupt end when Gable met and married Josephine Dillon.

It was strange that Gable had called the most unlikely person a man could ever turn to for defense of his honor—the girl he jilted. But Franz was full of good will and served as a loyal friend in Gable's hour of need. She said that during the times they were not on stage in the stock company shows, she and Gable would live at her father's farm.

"We planned our marriage and decided on two children," Miss Doerfler said. "But Clark grew bored with me after he met Josephine Dillon. And one morning I learned by telephone he had married Miss Dillon."

The prosecution also brought four witnesses down from Oregon—U. Ernest Nelson, Chris Neilsen, and Margaret Liesure, of Portland, and M. T. Woodward, of Silverton; they established the fact that Clark was working in Oregon during the years Mrs. Norton said she was his mistress in England. Woodward smiled as he told from the witness stand that the great Clark Gable, a $2,000-a-week star now, was paid $3.20 a day in 1923. Nelson, who was president of the Silver Falls Lumber Company, greeted his former employee with a big grin.

"Say, Clark," Nelson smiled, "can you still cut trees? You can have your old job back any time you want it. You're the best dad-gummed woodchopper I ever had."

Clark grinned, "I'll say I can still chop wood. And I may take you up on that job offer some day."

The jury of twelve men took an hour and fifty-five minutes to reach a verdict against Mrs. Norton—guilty! Earlier the judge upheld a motion for a directed verdict of acquittal for co-defendant Smith, the private eye.

Mrs. Norton took the verdict calmly—and the possibility

of five years in prison, or a $10,000 fine, or both. However, her attorney, Maurice Levine, immediately appealed for a probationary sentence, which permitted Mrs. Norton to leave the country and never to return.

And it was granted. Mrs. Norton was deported to Canada and was never heard from again.

Soon afterward, Gable turned his attention to another woman—his second wife. The first step in that direction came on May 6, 1937, when Mrs. Gable took legal steps to collect a heftier slice of the cash his movies were pouring into Clark's coffers. Her attorney, Mendel Silberberg, went to see Gable's lawyer, Edward R. Young, to negotiate an amicable settlement that would enable his client to go on his way a carefree bachelor—or to marry Carole Lombard, as all Hollywood was betting.

Clark, who had pulled down $108,000 for his celluloid sex appeal in 1935, cited figures to show that up to May of 1937 he had parted with nearly $145,000 in order to reach a settlement with his wife; he said he had given Rhea two trust funds, one of $50,000 and another of $25,000, besides $15,000 in cash. In addition, she collected half his film salary for 1936, which amounted to $54,000 as her share. But Gable balked when it was suggested he fork over a larger portion of his earnings.

There was no immediate disposition of Rhea's efforts to grasp a bigger hunk of Clark's income, and discussions between the lawyers dragged on for many, many months.

Meanwhile, Clark continued to be seen more and more with Carole Lombard and considerably less often with other women. It became an academic matter in Hollywood by now that Clark's sole and abiding interest was in one girl and one girl alone—the sacred and profane Carole, who seemed to fill Gable's conception of what he wanted in a wife as close to perfection as anyone could.

During these months of his involvement with women, both famous and infamous, a new concept of acting and motion picture-making was rapidly being mapped elsewhere in a manner approaching nothing Gable or anyone else had ever known. In time this planning was to influence Gable's life and acting career, as well as the film industry's, as no movie production had ever done.

It was to be a twentieth-century fantasy, and Gable was to be its central character, around whom would evolve some of the most fantastic contretemps ever to figure in a film-making enterprise in all history; it would provide grounds for a divorce, be blamed for a couple of suicides, guide several women into matrimony, disrupt hundreds and thousands of social activities and gatherings, fill more newspaper columns than any event of world importance of the times, and split many households into daily debates over the selection of the woman who should play the lead opposite Clark Gable.

It began on June 3, 1936, with the delivery of a book by an agent of the Macmillan Company, the publishing house, to Katherine Brown, the representative for movie producer David O. Selznick, in New York. The book was an advance copy of a first novel by Margaret Mitchell with a title culled from Ernest Dowson's poem "Cynara."

Miss Brown read its 1,037 pages and was fascinated. She immediately phoned the telegraph office and ordered this wire sent to her boss:

"If you don't buy *Gone With the Wind* you're crazy."

It wasn't the way to speak to the boss, but the boss got the message. He rushed into negotiations and by July 30th a deal was made—Selznick had bought *Gone With the Wind* for $50,000. It wasn't the highest price ever paid in movie history but it was, for those days, a more-than-fair deal for a first novel.

Even before Selznick had completed his negotiations, the thousands upon thousands who read the book began to envision it as a gigantic and spectacular motion picture and, astonishingly enough, they visualized but one, and only one, actor—one actor alone as the central male character of the book.

An actor named Clark Gable . . .

# 10

## *Gone With the Wind*

WHEN SHERMAN TOOK AT-lanta late in 1864, hardly did he dream that seventy-five years later—not quite to the day—David O. Selznick would follow in his footsteps over the same fields once strewn with dead and dying and capture the great city again—but with one difference. Instead of breaking the heart of the Confederacy, the invader from the North this time would win it.

For that is precisely what Selznick did with *Gone With the Wind*—he took the South. And Clark Gable, playing the sneering, profiteering blockade-runner who loved and finally won the selfish, self-willed heroine of Margaret Mitchell's great historical novel, Scarlett O'Hara, headed the distinguished procession in the triumphant march through the

Southland with Selznick and the rest of the thousands who helped make *Gone With the Wind* the most astonishing production venture of its time. It was so magnificent, so vast in scope, so extensive in its impact and influence, so tremendous in its financial and casting profluencies, and so spectacular as to compel consideration as a social phenomenon.

There had never been anything like *Gone With the Wind* before. There has not been anything like it since.

When *Gone With the Wind* was bought by Selznick after that frenzied, unorthodox telegram from Katherine Brown, it was not more than two weeks before an entire nation knew a best-seller had been born. And in the great rush to swallow up the torrent of copies of the book that rolled off the publisher's presses, there was an incredible, if not fantastic, agreement among the millions of readers that only one man, and one man alone, could play Rhett Butler—Clark Gable. But who would be the black-haired, green-eyed, wasp-waisted Scarlett? Casting Scarlett became a national guessing game with participants from all forty-eight states as well as the then Territories of Alaska and Hawaii. It was a game Selznick enjoyed—for he wanted more than anything to have a perfect Scarlett, and to him no one in Hollywood seemed quite suitable for the role.

But casting was not Selznick's immediate problem. There is much more to making movies than buying the book and picking players. A script is the immediate and indispensable objective. Costumes and properties must be obtained. Sets have to be designed and built. There were also such matters as décor, the Georgian accents that had to be transplanted into the voices of the cast, and the musical scores. Contracts for raw materials had to be negotiated. Labor was needed. None of these essential steps could be neglected or delayed while the search for the cast—even its starring heroine, Scarlett—was in progress.

Selznick designated Sidney Howard to write the script in late 1936. It was an enormous job for it presented more than the usual number of problems that ordinary script writing poses; Miss Mitchell's book had to be translated, or adapted, into a screenplay with scrupulous and unstinting accuracy. That was what Selznick demanded. The first draft was drawn up on February 20, 1937. Yet the stamp of approval was not put on the final shooting script until more than two years later, February 27, 1939. In the meantime, other talented writers were called to lend their know-how to the preparation of the script, writers like Oliver H. P. Garrett and Jo Swerling. And there were others, too.

Finally, out of all the hectic and furious-paced writing that was poured out for *Gone With the Wind*, there evolved six complete scripts, six incomplete scripts, one "second-unit" script that was for the guidance of the crews on location, and four scripts incorporating retakes, added scenes, and "wild" lines.

Still another script was prepared for the assistant director, to show the number of pages of script for each scene, the number of scenes in each sequence, the properties required, construction needs, music, other sound effects, wardrobe changes, the talking parts, the number of extras, the bit parts.

Before the last line of script was done, the collective efforts of the Selznick writing team had filled seven large filing cabinet drawers with story material on *Gone With the Wind.* There has never been so much writing in any opus for the screen before or since. *Rebecca,* a later production that Selznick made, only required the space of half a drawer for comparable material. That's how enormous *GWTW* was.

In its final version—the one the nation finally saw on the silver screen—the picture emerged with 685 scenes consisting of 20,017 words of dialogue. And while Selznick maintained an understandable blackout on the cost of the script, experts have guessed that it cost at least four or five times the $50,000 paid the author, Miss Mitchell.

Meanwhile, during the frenetic writing sequences in Hollywood, other fronts were ablaze with activity as *Gone With the Wind* was being "pieced" together. The costume designer, Walter Plunkett, was off to the South to seek inspiration and material. His work, begun a month after the novel was bought, took him to the Smithsonian Institution for a study and gathering of documented historical facts to support the book and its scenes; he later went to Atlanta, Savannah, Charleston, and New Orleans.

All told, the wardrobe alone for *Gone With the Wind* totaled an astronomical $153,818, which included labor. The women's costumes accounted for the bulk of the figure— $98,154. And these were late Depression Day costs, when materials and labor were at their lowest. If the effort were to be duplicated today, the cost might well reach a million dollars!

At the same time, efforts had to be directed into other areas—the preparation of properties was a major undertaking. This meant that prop men—guided by a staff of researchers who jealously perform their work as if one minor error in chronology is much more serious than an actor's flub—had to assemble the vast paraphernalia that was to be used in the film.

Involved in the search, or manufacture, were such items as carpet-bags of genuine Brussels carpet, fifty dozen peacock feathers for fly-swashers, children's toys of the period, Civil War locomotive and coaches, hundreds of John Brown pikes (iron-headed seven-foot staves), an 1860 sawmill, shovels shaped like spades found on playing cards, cast-iron lampposts—and even a coffin! These were but a sample of the 1,250,000 props required for *GWTW*. And the cost: a cool $96,758.

Remember this. All these preparations were now under way—and Selznick still had not found his Scarlett O'Hara. Clark Gable's co-star, about whom the whole picture would spin, was yet the objective of a world-wide search, with no clue as to her identity.

But the groundwork went on. The script, which was also in the hands of the production designer, William Cameron Menzies, and the art director, Lyle Wheeler, was being translated into scenes at the same times. First the scenes had to be discussed. An oral portrait was painted of each scene. Then each one was made into a sketch—until 3,000 sketches were completed, a virtual duplication of Walt Disney's techniques and processes which employ background, camera angles, close-ups, and long shots, as well as color application.

As in the case of everything else that went into the production—no matter how small and insignificant it may have seemed—the sketches had to be submitted to Selznick, who in turn passed them on to the interior decorator, Joseph Platt. The original 3,000 sketches were crude designs, but they were graphic enough to indicate the scenes. From these, the desirable ones were extracted and were then prepared as careful line and color drawings; architects' elevations and blueprints followed. In the end, two hundred sets were actually designed. Of these, ninety were finally selected and constructed.

The enormity of the job is graphically illustrated in the scene of Atlanta recreated as it was in Civil War Days—a set that consisted of fifty-three buildings and seven thousand feet of streets!

Atlanta was rebuilt—and the heroine of the Civil War historical novel was still not found! Where was Scarlett O'Hara? Who would be the lucky actress to fill her tiny shoes?

That was still Selznick's headache, but he had yet other, more immediate problems to contend with. There was the matter of landscaping the sets. The "greens" department—a subsidiary of the prop department—went off on a search of the Los Angeles suburbs for the flora required to lend the touch of the Old Southern plantations on the make-believe scenes rising like a nostalgic reminder of the bygone on Hollywood locations. A couple of dogwoods in someone's backyard, a magnolia tree on another's front lawn, a peach tree here, a few other varieties there—all of them acquired by private and separate negotiations with the owners, a huge and time-consuming undertaking in itself. Then followed problems of transplanting the trees and of their "conversion" in some cases. For example, apple trees, which do not bloom in Southern California, had to be created from dogwoods which were decorated with appropriate blossoms of paper. Still more trees, like huge elms, had to be transplanted from the hills, as well as others.

Then real sod had to be hauled in (phony greensward cannot pass the faithful chromatic representation of Technicolor on the screen); the red clay of Georgia was reproduced by a workable mixture of ground brick dust and paint.

Altogether, the sets cost $197,877.

By December of 1938, all these details had been attended to. *Gone With the Wind* was in the works.

But what of Scarlett O'Hara? Who was going to be Clark Gable's co-star?

Director George Cukor, who up to that stage had not had opportunity to direct a single motion or movement or word of dialogue in the film, returned from an extensive nine-state tour south of the Mason-Dixon line in search of a Scarlett. He had interviewed one hundred candidates, but had not succeeded in finding the heroine he sought. The same sad story came from Oscar Serlin, who had searched in vain through the North and East, and the same from Charles Morrison, the field agent for the West. And just in case Cukor might have overlooked any Southern belles, Maxwell Arnow conducted his own talent hunt in the Confederacy without luck.

A total of 1,400 candidates had been interviewed and twenty-eight of them were given screen tests that ran up 149,000 feet of black and white film, 13,000 in Technicolor, at a cost of $92,000. But it was all wasted effort. Scarlett O'Hara was not among these hopefuls.

Now there was a problem. David Selznick was faced with an incongruous production hurdle that had to be jumped before construction could begin on the city of Atlanta. As any amateur historian knows, Atlanta was burned down during the Civil War. And Selznick had to do that to maintain the realism of Miss Mitchell's book. There was one difference in the way Selznick did it. He burned the city down before he built it!

Although the burning of Atlanta does not come until late in Miss Mitchell's book, the story did not have the restricted 40-acre back lot that Selznick had at his studio. So he set the fire first. Lee Zavitz, filmland's arson expert, was called in. The situation was explained to him. The lot at the time consisted of a number of hangover sets—buildings from *King of Kings* and *Garden of Allah,* a panorama of little old New York, a jail, and some others.

"We'll put false fronts on these buildings, fronts designed

after our own Civil War plans for Atlanta," Selznick told Zavitz. "Then you burn it down. After that we'll clean the debris and build Atlanta for the picture."

"Shouldn't be hard," Zavitz said. "Under the smoke haze it should look like the real thing."

The false fronts were hastily erected on the relic sets. Meanwhile Zavitz had a network of pipelines laid behind and above the facades through which some 15,000 gallons of fuel oil would pass to feed the fire—then water to douse it after the scenes were shot.

On December 10, 1938, all was in readiness. Seven Technicolor cameras were spotted on the lot. Everything was set.

The fire was started and it burned into the night. Working at a furious pace to capture all the vivid scenes of the blazing inferno, thousands of feet of film were shot. Cost: $26,000.

The next day, crews of laborers started to clear the charred "city" and soon afterward the carpenters and other workmen went in to build Atlanta.

On January 26, 1939, actual shooting began on a tiny set that had Scarlett O'Hara—for the search for Scarlett had finally ended, less than two weeks before (more on that in the next chapter)—clutching a bedpost while old Mammy yanked her corset strings. The order to start was shouted by director George Cukor. A few weeks later, the orders were called by Victor Fleming, who had taken over after Cukor's departure "by mutual consent." Later Sam Wood, of *Good-bye, Mr. Chips* fame, took Fleming's place for a while, serving as a second unit man. As the production grew more complicated, more difficult, other directors were called in to lend their talents.

While to the average visitor on the various sets things may have seemed confused and even chaotic, the directors worked so efficiently and effectively that production went precisely according to schedule—140 days.

The statistics at the conclusion of all the combined efforts of all the people involved were staggering.

Altogether, 4,400 persons had worked directly on the film, including 2,400 extras. Their salaries alone totaled $108,469. All told salaries of the cast ran to $566,788, about 14 per cent of the total cost. Add to this a million and a half dollars for labor—one-million man-hours at $1.50 an hour. That was over two millions just for salaries.

Some incidentals: 700 bottles of grease paint, 300 yards of crepe hair for 700 mustaches and 500 pairs of sideburns.

Other costs, such as wardrobe, sets, and properties consumed about 12 per cent of the budget; script and direction, 13 per cent; raw materials, including film, 8 per cent; lighting, transportation, and other services, 7 per cent. Miscellaneous expenses which took in all the rest—except salaries which ran 39 per cent—added up to 21 per cent.

All told it cost $3,957,000—without a cent yet spent for publicity and exploitation, nor the price tag on four hundred prints at $1,000 each—$400,000.

Speaking of the film, when shooting was finished there were 475,000 feet of exposed film which cost $109,974. If the entire total had been shown on the screens it would have run a solid eighty-three hours!

Edited—to do this required 2,500 hours in the projection room and 16,000 hours in the cutting room—the picture came down to 20,500 feet which brought "Gone With the Wind" down to a mere three hours and forty-five minutes' playing time—a playing time that still stands to this day as an all-time world's record for the length of a movie.

In the first year of its roadshow presentation, an estimated 25,000,000 people saw the film—an unprecedented turnout. More unusual was the fact that about one-third of those who saw the picture expressed hopes of seeing it again. Over fifty million declared their earnest intention to see the film.

All in all, GWTW shattered records practically everywhere it played in the United States and even outside the country, as in England, where it ran eighty-four days at London's Empire Theatre and was simultaneously presented at the Ritz and the Palace. It held up for eight weeks in the Liberty Theatre in Sydney, Australia, playing day and date with the St. James; a month at the Plaza in Capetown and a month in Johannesburg, South Africa. In Bombay and Calcutta, India, it ran five weeks, and at the Roxy in Shanghai and the Capitol in Singapore it had forty-three and twenty-one-day runs, respectively.

By 1954, GWTW had begun its fifth coast-to-coast hurricane and the box offices were still deluged by anxious film fans, both those who had seen it before and many who had not.

By 1961, Metro-Goldwyn-Mayer had again decided to release the film for simultaneous showings across the country and even before it had started its run the bookkeepers and accountants at Metro had figured that this $4,357,000 production had brought in nearly $60,000,000—another world record.

No matter which way you look at it, Gone With the Wind was, still is, and always will be the granddaddy of all the gigantic and spectacular films that Hollywood has sent forth into the world.

But, really, GWTW is hardly a film any more.

It is a social phenomenon—and an American tradition.

# 11

## *GWTW Can't Stop Marriage to Carole*

FROM THE MOMENT DAVID O.
Selznick announced he had bought Margaret Mitchell's book
for $50,000, America's film fans decided no man could play
Rhett Butler's part except one—their screen idol, Clark
Gable.

Curiously, this was a choice based on the public's emotions
and sentiment more than on logic. In reading Miss Mitchell's
masterpiece, the overwhelming majority were convinced the
author had sculpted her chief male character in the image of
filmland's leading hero. But neither Gable himself, nor the
public for that matter, had any reasonable grounds to believe
he was going to get the part.

Gable was a Metro-Goldwyn-Mayer star, under contract
to the studio with iron-clad clauses that specified his services
belonged exclusively to MGM. And *GWTW* had been bought
by Selznick, who was an independent producer. Logically,
then, it had to be assumed MGM would jealously withhold
the services of its star rather than glorify a rival film-maker.
But it didn't work that way.

Gable himself explained what finally happened.

"I knew what was coming the day Selznick phoned me.
Our talk was amicable. I did the sparring and he landed the
hard punches. David's idea was to make a separate deal, pro-
viding my studio would release me to make the picture. But
I didn't want the part and told David that. David nevertheless
insisted he would have me for the part. I thought my contract
was an ace in the hole. It specified that my services belonged
exclusively to Metro. I told that to David, adding on my own
that I was not interested in playing Rhett.

"That didn't stop David. Being a friend of long standing
and knowing him, I knew that it wouldn't. Selznick wouldn't
take no for an answer. He put his cards on the table."

"No actor has ever been offered the chance I'm giving
you," Selznick told Gable. "There's never been a more
talked-of role than Rhett."

"That's exactly my reason for turning you down," Clark
replied.

"I'm going to try to get you from MGM if I can. You're going to play Rhett—and you're going to like it. I give you my word you will be Rhett Butler, because you are in life the personification of Rhett Butler. No other man can play that role."

Gable, still not convinced he was made for the part, resignedly told Selznick to proceed with his intended negotiations with the studio. Clark was almost convinced MGM would never let him go.

"I never asked to play Rhett," Clark said. "I was one of the last to read the book. And out of curiosity I inquired and learned I was not Miss Mitchell's inspiration for creating Rhett. When she was writing her book, Hollywood never had heard of me, and I am certain Miss Mitchell was not interested in an obscure Oklahoma oil field worker, which I was at the time.

"In the interest of truth, I became a fan of Miss Mitchell's, with the rest of America, after going half-way through the book. It was good, too good in fact. Rhett was everything a character should be, and rarely is, concise and very real. He breathed in the pages of the book. He was flawless as a character study. He stood up under the most careful analysis, without exhibiting a weakness. That was the trouble.

"I realized that whoever played Rhett would be up against a stumbling block in this respect. Miss Mitchell had etched Rhett into the minds of millions of people, each of whom knew exactly how Rhett would look and act. It would be impossible to satisfy them all. An actor would be lucky to please even the majority. It wasn't that I didn't want to play Rhett. I did. No actor would entirely resist such a challenge. But the more popular Rhett became, the more I agreed with the gentleman who wrote, 'Discretion is the better part of valor.'

"To make sure that I hadn't erred in my first impression, I read *Gone* again. It convinced me more than ever that Rhett was too much for any actor to tackle in his right mind. But I couldn't escape him."

Gable was an immovable object—but Selznick was an irresistible force. He convinced Metro that Gable was the only actor who could play Rhett Butler—and a deal was swung.

"I could have put up a fight," Gable said. "I didn't. I'm glad I didn't."

So Clark Gable was picked. But what of Scarlett O'Hara? Who was going to play the selfish, hoydenish, slant-eyed pedigreed bitch who tackled life with an unconquerable determination born of a creamy complexion and tiger's claws?

In time, the question came to take on the proportions of a national emergency. With the great talent search yielding nothing, and while the guessing game was at its height, Hollywood columnists and writers had a field day with their "exclusive" selections.

"I have learned directly from the front office that David O. Selznick has definitely decided Jean Arthur will be his Scarlett O'Hara," reported one famous columnist.

"Flash!" wrote a second noted Hollywood byliner a few days later. "Loretta Young is all picked for the role of Scarlett."

A few weeks later, a third columnist finally had gotten to the bottom of things. It wasn't going to be Jean Arthur nor Loretta Young.

"Bette Davis is going to be Scarlett O'Hara," it was written.

Now after a decent period of time had passed, the first columnist came back to shock her readers.

"Jean Arthur is not going to play Scarlett O'Hara—David Selznick has made up his mind that no one can fill Scarlett O'Hara's shoes but the one and only Norma Shearer."

And so it went. From Shearer back to Davis, then to Young and over to Arthur. Like a football being lateralled over the gridiron. About the only Hollywood star who wasn't mentioned was Shirley Temple. Too young, you know.

The problem was resolved dramatically one afternoon in December of 1938. Myron Selznick, David's brother, a leading Hollywood agent, walked into the producer's office guiding a beautiful young woman with a very slim figure. At the time, the fire scene had already been completed and Atlanta was being built.

David turned to greet Myron.

"I want you," Myron said, "to meet Scarlett O'Hara."

David smiled wearily, for he didn't always have a sense of appreciation for his brother's humor. David turned casually to the visitor, then did a double take.

"You know, Myron—you may be right!"

David ordered screen tests immediately.

And that was how Vivien Leigh came to be Scarlett O'Hara. But that isn't the whole story. Miss Leigh had been in a play in London when she first read *Gone With the Wind* and immediately she wanted to play Scarlett. She told other members of the cast, "If I ever go to Hollywood, it will be to play *Gone With the Wind.*"

They all laughed, Miss Leigh said. "They thought I was crazy."

In December of 1938, Miss Leigh came to the United States and intended to visit here for two weeks. Then she met Myron Selznick and she became Scarlett O'Hara. She signed her contract for *Gone With the Wind* on January 13, 1939. It was a Friday the 13th, an unlucky day—for the 1,399 discarded candidates for Scarlett's part.

The choice seemed to please everyone—everyone, that is, except the Hollywood actresses and the other hopefuls who had flunked out—and especially Gable. Not immediately, of course, because he didn't know Miss Leigh, who had never been in Hollywood. But it didn't take Gable long to find out about her acting talents once the shooting on *Gone With the Wind* began.

"I certainly am pleased," Gable said. "Miss Leigh makes Scarlett so vividly lifelike that it makes my playing of Rhett such simpler than I had expected."

Gable's enthusiasm over Vivien Leigh lasted throughout the long and arduous filming. And when it was all over and the last foot of celluloid had been shot, Gable was still ecstatic over his leading lady, as well as the way the picture had gone.

Work, which had begun on the film on January 26, 1939, was about nearly fifty per cent completed by March, and on the seventh of that month developments came out of Las Vegas that threatened a sudden interruption in production.

After a brief hearing, Mrs. Rhea Gable had won a divorce!

And Clark Gable was now free to marry his glamorous Carole Lombard!

The question that came up at once to haunt the production chiefs on the *Gone With the Wind* set was: "How soon will Clark and Carole elope?" That they would elope was a distinct possibility, for Carole herself said that after word of the divorce reached her at the RKO studios where she was working on stills.

"Perhaps Clark and I will be married soon," Carole said. "We have made no plans really. Clark is working in *Gone With the Wind*, but when he gets a few days off and I am not busy, perhaps we'll sneak away and have the ceremony performed."

Clark himself was less voluble. "We have made no plans for the time or place," he declared.

The way to wed was cleared when Rhea, now 48, received the divorce after a five-minute private hearing before Judge William E. Orr. Property settlements and other preliminaries to the divorce, for which Gable paid Rhea $286,000—plus income tax—were arranged six weeks previously, before Mrs. Gable went to Las Vegas to establish residence for the divorce proceedings.

And, so, Clark Gable had achieved bachelor status once again. But there was no question in anyone's mind that it could not last. The only question was how long it would be before he married Carole.

Only Clark and Carole had the answer to that—and it was

to come with a suddenness and a swiftness that would surprise even their closest friends. It happened like this—

On the morning of March 29th, 1939, all the movie newshounds, who had been keeping Clark and Carole under close surveillance in Hollywood, were called to San Francisco to cover the preview of *The Story of Alexander Graham Bell*.

Unknown to his many friends, Clark arranged to have a few days off from *Gone With the Wind*. Carole did the same at RKO. Then Clark and Carole hopped into his long cream-colored roadster, picked up Otto Winkler, an MGM studio publicity representative, and sped away to Kingman, Arizona.

Late in the afternoon, Viola Olsen, the county clerk in the little Arizona town, was goggle-eyed as the film stars, whom she immediately recognized, walked in. Shy as any prospective bridegroom, Clark applied for a license and after it was granted he asked Miss Olsen:

"Can you recommend someone to marry us?"

"Yes, sir," replied Miss Olsen. "The Reverend Kenneth Engle, the pastor of the First Methodist Episcopal Church."

A few minutes later, the Reverend Mr. Engle tied the knot and Clark and Carole sped off to Boulder, Nevada, to spend their honeymoon.

Before leaving, Clark turned reporter and called the MGM press bureau to give the details of the wedding. Clark and Carole also fired off wires to friends at the studio and elsewhere announcing they'd done it. One of the messages was directed to William Randolph Hearst, the publisher.

"Married this afternoon," it said. "Carole and Clark."

For Carole, who was then 30—eight years younger than Clark—marriage to the handsome idol of the film world was the greatest happiness in her life. And for Gable, who had been through two marriages to older women, this try at matrimony was the culmination of a dream—the dream of marrying the only girl who seemed to be everything he wanted in a wife.

"They are the perfect match," was the way the columnists and writers put it. "They were meant for each other—this will be Hollywood's happiest marriage . . . It's made in heaven . . . It'll last forever . . ."

Forever—that's a long time.

For Carole and Clark, unfortunately, the future had to wait. There was the present to consider. *Gone With the Wind* had to be finished before they could even think about a honeymoon of any duration. They could only spend one night away, that night in Boulder. The next day they motored back to Hollywood—into the surge of a hundred newsmen and photographers. So great was the crush of reporters and lensmen that the poor, harried MGM press department hardly knew what to do. In desperation, it threw itself on the mercy of Clark and Carole, pleading with them to solve the problem.

Like the good scouts they were, Clark and Carole agreed to meet the newshounds in two shifts, one in the morning and another in the afternoon. In between, Clark and Carole dined with her mother, Mrs. Elizabeth Peters, in her Hollywood home. That night, Clark and Carole began their housekeeping in Carole's Beverly Hills apartment so he would be close to the studio. They didn't have the time to move into Clark's new ranch home in Encino, California. The next day he was back at work on *Gone With the Wind.*

The days and weeks passed swiftly and soon filming on the epic masterpiece of the motion picture world was finished; its premiere was set—in the very city of its inspiration, Atlanta.

It was the night of December 15, 1939, that a new generation of Atlantans—and a few of the old—relived their history as Hollywood moved to Georgia's capital city to stage an extravaganza of unequalled proportions.

For days and weeks Atlanta had been in a state of high-pitched excitement in anticipation of the local spectacular. Newspapers served up bulky souvenir editions which restored the latent spirit of the Confederacy with precise and unerring accuracy. The editions even carried grave instructions on how to give the rebel yell.

The theatre chosen for the gargantuan premiere was the Loew's Grand off the little square where Peachtree, Pryor and Forsyth Streets meet. The front of the theatre was redone with a reproduction in wood of the Greek-columned mansion, Twelve Oaks, in which Scarlett O'Hara had lived.

Two hours before the scheduled premiere, the area was roped off by four hundred guardsmen and details of State troopers and city police. Thousands had to be held behind the lines formed outside the theatre where clearings had to be established so the stars of the picture, as well as the author, Margaret Mitchell, could pass through.

The festive air was captured by the girls and women of Atlanta who came dressed in period costumes with hoop skirts, basques, long black lace gloves, and antebellum miniatures and other family heirlooms. They were the ushers and hostesses. The men, wearing black neckerchiefs and fawn-colored garments like the beaux of the 1860s, were the ushers, too.

A blinding play of light illuminated the Twelve Oaks set and, like a typical Hollywood opening, brilliant searchlights sent up their beams criss-crossing in the black sky above.

The crush was at its worst when Clark Gable, accompanied by Carole Lombard, reached the theatre. The guardsmen, who formed an iron-like human chain, strained to their maximum to withstand the tremendous pressure of the mobs; women screamed hysterically, men shouted themselves hoarse. Mayor

Hartsfield himself had gone to pick up Clark and Carole earlier and had taken them on a dignitary's tour of Atlanta, before depositing them at the Georgian Terrace Hotel, where they and the other prominent visitors were registered for their stay.

The crowning moment of the excitement outside the theatre came when Gable threw up his hands to the crowd to command their silence. As they responded, Gable said, "This is Margaret Mitchell's night and Atlanta's night. I want to see the picture just as you see it. Please, Atlanta, allow me to see *Gone With the Wind* tonight just as a spectator."

Indeed it was Margaret Mitchell's night—but it was everyone's night, too. It was Clark Gable's and Carole Lombard's, who was moved to tears by her pride in her husband; it was Vivien Leigh's night, and Leslie Howard's night, and Olivia deHavilland's night. It was also David O. Selznick's night and Victor Fleming's night.

It was a night to remember.

A little more than a month later, on the night of December 19, 1939, it was New York's turn to cheer and celebrate its premiere of *Gone With the Wind*. The film had its opening simultaneously in the Capitol and Astor Theatres on Broadway. Thousands mobbed the Great White Way to make the double-barreled premiere one of the most memorable of all time.

And through these great rounds of public receptions, what did the critics have to say?

The critics unanimously applauded and cheered; they were —for the first time—at a loss for adjectives to dress up their raves.

Typical is the review written by Frank S. Nugent for the haughty, lofty, august New York *Times* (which, incidentally, had covered the Atlanta opening with its great Pulitzer Prize-winning reporter, Meyer Berger). Nugent opened his review like this:

Understatement has its uses too, so this morning's report on the event of last night will begin with the casual notation that it was a great show . . . Is it the greatest motion picture ever made? Probably not, although it is the greatest motion mural we have seen and the most ambitious film-making venture in Hollywood's spectacular history . . . by any and all standards, Mr. Selznick's film is a handsome, scrupulous and unstinting version of the 1,037-page novel, matching it almost scene for scene with a literalness that not even Shakespeare or Dickens were accorded in Hollywood, casting it so brilliantly one would have to know the history of the production not to suspect that Miss Mitchell had written her story just to provide a vehicle for the stars already assembled under

Mr. Selznick's hospitable roof. To have treated so long a book with such astonishing fidelity required courage—the courage of a producer's convictions and of his pocketbook, and yet, so great a hold has Miss Mitchell on her public, it might have taken more courage still to have changed a line or scene of it.

Nugent was high in his praise of Gable, Miss Leigh, Leslie Howard, and Miss deHavilland, as well as the others in the cast.

For Clark Gable, his performance as Rhett Butler, gave him new stature, new eminence, new greatness in the sparkling heavens of Hollywood, for he had proved beyond doubt his ability and innate talent as an actor—the biggest attraction in Hollywood, or the world, by far.

He was the greatest, and by far.

After Clark and Carole came back to Hollywood from the Atlanta premiere, everyone was talking about the picture and the great celebration. Everyone was raving about the reception. Everyone, that is, but Clark. All he could talk about was Carole—about how warmly she had been received in Atlanta. He was like a schoolboy gushing about his first girlfriend.

"You should have seen the way they looked at Carole," Gable would say. "You never saw anybody so beautiful."

There was no doubt about it—Clark Gable was in love, deeply and insensibly in love with Carole Lombard, a woman who returned his love completely but who, at the same time, managed to belong to herself. She was the woman for Clark Gable—a woman worth possessing forever.

But forever is so long—and for Clark and Carole, their forever would be mercilessly, tragically, tearfully short . . .

# 12

## *The Legendary Love of Clark and Carole*

ALL HIS LIFE, CLARK GABLE lived as though he believed his luck couldn't hold out. He was wrong. His luck held out—all except once. . . .

Clark and Carole started life together after the hysteria surrounding *Gone With the Wind* had died down. But it was only the beginning of a hysterical existence, one that would be filled with ingenious idiocies, spectacular pranks, incredible shenanigans; also deep, warm, and abiding love—and, finally, heartbreaking tragedy.

All the way through, from start to finish, they had a fun-filled life together, right from the day they packed for the honeymoon and headed for Lower California. That was January 25, 1940—an important day in Clark Gable's life in another respect. That was the day he signed a new contract with Metro-Goldwyn-Mayer, a seven-year pact that started Clark off at $5,000 a week and increases that gave the "King of Hollywood" a total of $2,000,000 over the period. It was one of the biggest money deals in film history up to then.

When Clark returned home after inking the new pact, he found Carole waiting. The station wagon was packed for the long journey. It was loaded down with everything, from sleeping blankets and cooking utensils to guns and fishing tackle. They were going into wild, sparsely-settled country, a region of Ensenada, which is cut by arroyos and low mountains. The station wagon was fitted with a sixty-five gallon gas tank for the long trip.

"Did we forget anything?" Clark asked Carole as they fancied the overloaded station wagon.

"If we did, we can always forget about it, Moose," Carole quipped. "We've got enough gear to stake us out for a year."

They drove off, waving goodbye to the neighbors. It was to be a month's honeymoon—a month the studio gave Clark for signing. And it was a month that Clark and Carole spent in supreme happiness, doing the things that Clark loved—hunting and fishing and camping. These were the pastimes that Carole had promised herself to take up, and enjoy, and share with her husband.

During their stay, Metro publicity man Otto Winkler, a personal friend of Clark's and a neighbor, flew down to the Hattie Hamilton Ranch, 115 miles south of Ensenada, expecting to meet Gable and his wife and shoot some pictures of the vacationing stars. But Clark and Carole had gone off to the LaBrea Gun Club, about 15 miles away. Winkler waited and when they failed to return by dusk he sent an SOS to Hollywood. Big black headlines flashed across the country:

*Gable Missing with Carole on Hunt in Mexico.*

Even before the editions had been run off, Clark and Carole returned. They had been duck hunting and had shot fifty birds.

"Got any ideas what we can do with these ducks?" Clark asked Winkler. Otto threw up his hands. Carole was just as much at a loss. Then Clark thought of something.

"Let's fly up home with Otto and surprise everyone with a

duck dinner," Clark offered.

"Okay, Pappy," Carole enthused, "you got an idea going."

They flew to Hollywood in Winkler's plane, made a hurried round of friends' homes, presented their gifts of game, then winged back to Lower California. When the month was up, they returned to Hollywood to a magnificent 22-acre ranch Clark had bought in Encino, a 45-minute drive from the MGM studios. This was home—a home that Carole and Clark would make into a legendary showplace of their mutual love for each other and their warm and tender affection for the simple life they sought to live.

But most of all, the Encino ranch would be a place long to be remembered for the zany and hilarious antics that Clark and Carole played on each other. They put big production value into their hoddy-doddies. There wasn't a night that Carole could go to bed knowing for sure whether she'd wake up to find Clark, or an old geezer with a long, white beard under the quilt by her side.

Once, shortly after the honeymoon, Carole caught a bad case of poison ivy. She had to wear a medicinal face-mask. One evening Clark came home to find a gutta-percha facsimile of Joan Crawford's face on the pillow where Carole's face should have been!

Not long after they returned from their honeymoon, Clark bought a trailer so Carole could accompany him on his future hunting jaunts with his all-male hunting club. Carole was so much of a sport that the other members made an exception for her.

One night, Carole was in the trailer and Clark, playing cards with the boys, started to yawn and announced he was ready to turn in. Five minutes after he left, there was a loud crash and everyone ran out to investigate. The trailer, jolted off its blocks, had collapsed on the ground. Clark and Carole, smothered in blankets, were laughing so hard they couldn't talk.

Although Carole was notably a "boudoir" girl, she was determined to make herself over into the image of Gable's dreamgirl. She learned to ride and to fire a gun and to take her sleep on the hard ground of the great outdoors, uncomplainingly, unflinchingly. Gable loved her all the more for her devotion to his kind of life and thrilled watching Carole make good at it.

When Carole returned to work at the Culver City studio for RKO's *Mr. and Mrs. Smith,* co-starring Robert Montgomery, she was greeted on her first day back by a huge sound truck whose sides were emblazoned with the message: "Culver City Welcomes Mrs. Rhett Butler!" Mounted on the sound truck, dressed in cutaway coat, high silk hat, a Smith Brothers beard, a cauliflower in his buttonhole, posing as "mayor" of Culver City, was Lew Smith, Clark's stand-in and good friend. When Carole's car crossed the city line, the "mayor" stopped her car, bowed, and presented her with a huge bouquet. It was a bouquet of onions, leeks, parsley, and a very old artichoke as the corsage's centerpiece. Carole took one good look at the "mayor," yanked off his beard, and commented:

"You've got more ham in you than Pappy!"

Carole put her brain to work overtime to figure out a comeback. In time she dreamed up a magnificent scheme. She would charter a plane to fly over the *Comrade X* company in which Clark was playing the lead. The pilot would drop thousands of leaflets carrying the unhappy words "Remember Parnell!" Carole was sure Clark's face would turn red, and she was hoping it would happen while he had Hedy Lamarr in his arms. *Parnell* was one of Gable's flops.

But Carole was frustrated in her aerial stunt by the Bureau of Air Commerce. Against regulations, they told her. But since she had already had the leaflets printed, she decided to hire some handbill distributors who posted themselves at the studio front entrance and passed out the "Parnell" reminders. Gable's face did turn red, but he found no fault with Carole's criticism. He admitted himself, "It's one of my worst pictures."

When Carole went to the hospital for an appendectomy, Clark paid her a visit one afternoon. He went to her room, bent over the bed, and was about to peck her cheek when, lo and behold! a strange pair of brown eyes glanced up at him with a look of incredulity. The expression on the woman's face then became a mask of heavenly joy. She struggled to get up and throw her arms around Gable. He barely got out of the room in time.

Moments later, in the hall where he was walking around aimlessly to find Carole's room, a nurse came down the hall laughing her head off. She stopped to tell another nurse what had happened.

"The husband of that woman in there just stopped me and he was all white-faced and shaking. He had just been in to see his wife. He think's she's delirious. She claims that Clark Gable came into her room, bent over the bed, and almost kissed her."

Clark finally tracked down Carole—in the room next to the one occupied by the woman with the brown eyes. Carole swore up and down to Clark that she had nothing to do with switching rooms with the woman next door.

On their first wedding anniversary, Carole decided to bring Clark's present to the MGM studio, where he was toiling with Spencer Tracy and Hedy Lamarr in *Boom Town*. Carole came over to have lunch with her one-year bridegroom in his portable dressing room, got there before the lunch hour, and spent a fast half hour fixing up the room with yards and yards of white satin ribbon, tulle and flowers. In one corner she arranged a nest, deposited an ostrich egg with the word "Parnell" painted across it in big, red letters.

Clark's anniversary gift to Carole was a beautiful gown, designed by Adrian. The material was rich and sheer and shimmering—but the design was all newspaper headlines: "Parsons Pans Lombard!" "Lombard Flops Again!" "Lombard Limited—And How!" "Critics Cauterize Carole!" and more.

Carole got back at Clark quickly for that one. That night when her former secretary, Fieldsie, now Mrs. Walter Lang, gave a swank anniversary party for the couple, Carole wore the gown to the party!

Life was a lark to Carole Lombard. She seemed absolutely incapable of gloom and it was her daffiness as much as her striking beauty and formidable figure that appealed to Clark Gable.

Carole was forever pursuing the gag, and more often than not, Clark was the victim. But sometimes, the joke was on others. The parties tossed at the ranch were ideal for Carole's antics.

Once, even before she was married to Clark, Carole invited a passel of Hollywood bigwigs to her house for what had been billed in advance as a posh and very correct dinner party. When the guests trooped in, decked out in white ties and mink, Carole, dead-panned, led them into the drawing room. Which was fine, except that Carole had removed every stick of furniture and piled the floor knee-deep with hay.

At another party, this one at the ranch, Carole decided that the Gables should form a "jive" orchestra like Mickey Rooney's and Jackie Cooper's and some of the other kids around Hollywood. So as the guests showed up, one by one, they were met at the door by Clark and Carole who handed each of them a musical instrument. The orchestra finally shaped up with Clark at the drums, Carole playing trumpet, Spencer Tracy tangling with a bass fiddle, Robert Taylor in the brass section, and Fred MacMurray tooting a saxophone.

Clark loved every moment of life with Carole, who was life itself. Carole, with her buoyancy, her frivolity, her everlasting gaiety, matched Gable's own zest for living.

As for Carole, Gable was the fulfillment of her own life's dreams. In Clark, she found the one man on whom she could lean, a strong, powerful, masterly man to enfold her and protect her.

Adela Rogers St. Johns, a close personal friend of both Gable and Miss Lombard, tells of a time shortly after the newlyweds had moved into their ranch house at Encino.

"Carole," Miss St. Johns relates, "got annoyed about a plumber who hadn't done whatever it was he said he'd do.

She let loose with words that smelled of brimstone.

"All of a sudden, she felt strong fingers on her wrists. She was jerked around brutally and found herself looking up into the kind of cold eyes with which Gable usually stared over a drawn gun.

" 'Listen, baby,' he said in a when-you-call-me-that-smile voice, 'if there is any cussing in this family, I'm man enough to do it myself.'

"The screen's favorite comedienne of the day tilted her head sideways so that the shining curtain of her blonde hair swung free. She stared up at him and then fell on his chest, flung her arms around his neck and began to weep wildly.

" 'Hi, honey,' Clark said, and through her sobs his bride said, 'I've waited a long time for somebody to do that. Oh, Clark, I am glad I love you. I'm glad I married you.' "

It was to Miss St. Johns, incidentally, that Carole Lombard explained her legendary use of the kind of language more commonly associated with drunken longshoremen.

"Smoke screen," Carole said. "Protective coloration and camouflage. If you're a young blonde around this man's town, you have to keep the wolf pack off somehow and if you know all them words, they figure you know your way around and they don't act so rough."

Carole's imprint on Hollywood was an indelible one and her career in the film capital began even before Gable's.

Carole, born Carol Jane Peters on October 6, 1909, in Fort Wayne, Ind., broke into the movies in a picture called *Marriage in Transit.* A steady stream of minor roles came along after *Marriage in Transit* and Carole was just beginning to attract the attention of some of Hollywood's more important producers when sudden and painful tragedy struck.

On a black, starless night, her car became involved in a shattering collision and Carole's face was hideously cut and torn. The doctors told her she would never again be beautiful. Her career seemed ended. For days, as she lay in the hospital bed, Carole remained sullenly mute, broken of spirit, as a deep dark morass engulfed her. But summoning the same gritty determination that had carried her that far in her career, she decided she could not and would not give up easily. She called in a well-known plastic surgeon who operated on her face, and although it took a year, she did in time return triumphantly to the screen. The scars were gone. If anything, she was more beautiful than ever. She had nothing to show for the accident but two almost invisible white lines on the side of her face.

On returning to the Fox studios, though, Carole found that her contract had elapsed and she had to start all over again from scratch. In time she signed for a series of Mack Sennet slapstick comedies and those, in turn, brought her to the attention of Paul Stein, a director for Pathé, who signed her for the leading role in *Show Folks.* Her future looked secure, but bad luck continued to trail the young actress. Her contract was allowed to lapse at Fox and she retrogressed to a bit player once more in what few roles she was able to land as a free-lance actress.

Nevertheless, in spite of her obscure roles, she began to build up a public following and a smidgeon of fame came her way. Not much, but enough—enough for Paramount to decide to give her a new contract. That was her break. She appeared in such productions as *Up Pops the Devil, No One Man, No More Orchids, I Take This Woman,* and *Ladies' Man.*

Soon she was co-starring with George Raft in *Bolero* and *Rumba,* with Bing Crosby in *We're Not Dressing,* with Gary Cooper in *Now and Forever,* and with William Powell in *My Man Godfrey.*

Other top, juicy film roles followed—*The Gay Bride, Lady by Choice, Hands Across the Table, Love Before Breakfast* among them—and her fame reached new heights when she starred in *Nothing Sacred,* a sophisticated comedy by Ben Hecht.

By the time she began dating Clark Gable, she was the top comedienne in Hollywood, as famous and wealthy, probably, as the big-eared guy she fell completely in love with.

Their marriage was as close to Paradise-on-earth as anything either had ever known. Slap-happy and funfilled but warm and tender, a team in the supreme ultimate meaning of the word. They filled each other's lives and each other's hearts. They loved each other and, happily, they suited each other.

"It's an extra dividend," Gable once said, "when you like the girl you're in love with."

And so their marriage rolled and rollicked along, but as it did, other things were happening in the world beyond Hollywood, ominous things. Hitler's great war machine was scorching the earth of Europe and America was drawing perilously closer to the war each day.

Then came December 7, 1941—and Pearl Harbor.

As countless other Americans did, Clark Gable and Carole Lombard offered their services. They communicated directly with President Roosevelt, whom they had known personally from several White House visits, and the President informed them they could best serve by doing exactly what they had been doing all along—entertaining.

Carole promptly launched a war bond tour, kicking it off in her home state of Indiana.

"I wish you could come too, Pappy," she sighed wistfully as she packed for the trip.

Clark wished he could, too, but he was working, and so he said "Take Otto, then I won't worry about you."

Otto was Otto Winkler, the Metro press agent, who lived with his wife, Jill, just down the hill from the Gables. They were two of the stars' closest friends.

Accompanied by Otto and her mother, Mrs. Elizabeth K. Peters, Carole embarked on a whirlwind bond-selling tour in which she swept through a dozen cities and sold some $2,-000,000,000 worth of defense bonds. The tour was an immense success and in mid-January of 1942, after appearing at a rally in Amarillo, Texas, Carole decided to come home.

The date was January 16, 1942.

A telegram reached Clark Gable, telling him the time of her plane's arrival.

The telegram added—and it was almost as though Carole were saying the words aloud in her husky smiling voice:

"Hey, Pappy, you better join this man's Army."

Gable pocketed the wire and swung into action. He was going to give his "Ma" the best welcoming home she'd ever seen. With the help of his long-time houseman, Martin, Clark set about the job of arranging the table. Carole's personal maid and Jean Garceau, her secretary-business manager and chatelaine of the ranch, arranged a jungle of flowers.

Gable grabbed the phone and asked the studio to send a car and chauffeur and a couple of men from the publicity department to handle Carole's arrival at the airport. Gable himself could never go to meet her in public because of the overpowering mob scenes the two of them together would create.

As the time of Carole's homecoming drew near, Gable sent Martin down the hill to fetch Jill Winkler. Her husband, Otto, naturally, would be coming home, too.

"It'll sure be nice to have Ma back," Gable said, creasing his leathery face into a broad smile at the thought. "Life without her around ain't hardly worth living."

A young man from publicity, Larry Barbier, was waiting at the airport for Carole's plane. When the scheduled arrival time had come and gone, Larry called Ralph Wheelwright at the studio and said:

"The plane's late but can't find out anything. You'd think the war was being fought next door. Carole and Otto and Carole's mother are the only civilians on the plane."

Wheelwright said:

"Call Clark and tell him it's late. Stick around and let me know."

A short while later Larry called Wheelwright and said cryptically:

"Ralph, the plane's down!"

Wheelwright phoned Eddie Mannix, the producer and Clark's close friend, and broke the news to him.

"Meet me," Mannix said. "We'll go to Clark's together."

At the ranch, Mannix, who had by now received additional information, said gravely to the ashen actor:

"Carole's plane is down in the mountains. We're going. You ready?"

"They've seen it," added Wheelwright. "It's on fire."

" . . . in the mountains?" Gable repeated tonelessly. "Yes, I'm ready."

Gable vanished into another room and returned with several sweaters.

"You fellows may need these," he said, handing them around. "It'll be cold in the mountains."

He walked over to Jill Winkler and put an arm around her.

"You stay here, Jill," he said softly. "Your mother'll come. Maybe—maybe it's all right. You start praying, will you?"

The men sped to Burbank and hopped a chartered plane for Las Vegas.

The Transcontinental & Western Airlines plane carrying Carole, her mother, Otto Winkler, the pilot, co-pilot, and seventeen servicemen, flying through the peaks that jut skyward between Nevada and California, had slammed into Table Mountain, about 30 miles west of Las Vegas. A posse operating out of the Las Vegas sheriff's office had sighted the burning wreckage 8,700 feet up the side of the mountain, about 100 feet below the crest.

As Gable, Mannix, and others who had joined them flew through the brilliant late-afternoon sky toward Nevada, a heavy pall of silence enveloped the plane.

In Las Vegas, they went to the sheriff's office while another posse was being formed for an ascent into the mountains.

The sheriff, seeing the big raw-boned actor, and noticing the anguish written on his face, asked uncertainly:

"Well now—you got anybody on this plane you're interested in, Mr. Gable?"

Clark's voice was perfectly natural as he replied, "Yes, my wife."

As the first light of dawn broke in the Eastern sky on that first morning after he arrived, Gable turned to the sheriff and said, "We can go now."

But the sheriff, who'd apparently thought about it, and decided it would be best if Gable were spared the grisly sights that were certain to be awaiting him.

"We'd a lot rather—it's a mean trip, Mr. Gable, and—we don't know what we're going to find," he said. "Lots easier for us if you'd stay here. We'll do our best and be back as quick as we can."

Gable protested but in the end decided the sheriff was right. He joined Spencer Tracy who'd flown up to be with his old friend.

Eddie Mannix made the gruelling ascent with the posse, tearing his feet on the craggy, snow-covered precipitous incline. He saw Carole—or what remained of her; a strand of hair, a few trinkets, a pair of earrings, a burnt script lying near her hand.

The ascent and descent took three days. The bodies were carried down on pack mules. During the wait, Clark worked tirelessly in the camp, cooking over the outdoor fire and serving to the men who were part of the search team. One gnarled old desert rat had no teeth and was having trouble chewing. Gable stuck a $100 bill into a deputy's hand and said, "Buy the guy some teeth."

Eddie Mannix was the first of the rescue party to talk to Gable. "We found the plane," he said. "There weren't any survivors."

"I—know," Clark said softly. "I'm glad you were there, Eddie."

Gable had shed no tears, asked for no sympathy, and was unapproachable. On the final day there, when the campfires died, he wandered off into the darkness alone.

A laborer who had helped recover the bodies watched him and shook his head.

"There," he said, "goes one hell of a lot of man."

While in Las Vegas, Gable received a telegram he kept and cherished until his own death.

Carole was our friend [it read], our guest in happier days.

She brought a great deal of joy to all who knew her and to the millions who knew her only as a great artist. She gave unselfishly of her time and talent to serve her government in peace and in war. She loved her country.

She is and always will be a star, one we shall never forget nor cease to be grateful to. Deepest sympathy.

It was signed Franklin Delano Roosevelt.

Gable returned to Hollywood and arranged for a double funeral for Carole and her mother.

After that, Gable wasn't the same. Deprived of the buoyant, vibrant woman who had filled his life to overflowing for thirty-four unforgettable months, he slipped into a musing limbo fragrant with memories of Carole.

Months dragged past, and Gable completed the picture he was then working on, entitled, ironically, *Somewhere I'll Find You*. Restlessness grew in him, and he found the war more and more disturbing, and, perhaps, compelling.

Finally, he picked up the phone and put in a call to an old friend, General "Hap" Arnold.

"Hap," he said, "I want to enlist. Just tell me what to do."

# 13

## *Army Days*

IT WAS INEVITABLE THAT Clark Gable would answer the call to the colors in his nation's most perilous moment. It was inevitable, even had Carole Lombard lived. War had come, holding the world in its bloody grip.

Clark Gable, with his huge strength, his blazing free spirit, his deep abiding love for the land that had given him so much, was both ready and eager to join the struggle.

Actually, he had often talked with Carole in their Encino ranch house about his hopes of enlisting. He wasn't sure any of the services would have him, at least not as he wanted to serve—as an enlisted fighting man. He was 41 years old and safely past the age limit. He could, he knew, apply for and receive a commission for some soft, Stateside entertainment duty, but Gable, being Gable, would have no part of that. As he and Carole planned it, he would try to join the Army as a private and then, if he qualified, aim for Officer Candidate School. If he did receive an officer's commission it would be because he earned it, not because he was "King Gable."

In the bleak months following Carole's death, Gable methodically set about putting his affairs in order. He completed work on *Somewhere I'll Find You,* fulfilling his obligations to the studio.

When everything was in order, Gable consulted with "Hap" Arnold about enlisting, and in June of 1942 he flew to Washington, applied for duty in the Army Air Force, and underwent his physical examination at Bolling Field.

The War Department took his application under advisement and two months later ordered him to appear for induction.

On August 12, 1942, in the Federal Courthouse in Los Angeles, the King of Hollywood became a private in "this man's Army." He was Private Clark Gable, serial number 19125047, and a whole new life lay ahead of him.

The past was gone. The easy, laughing life of the most famous actor in the world was mothballed for as long as Uncle Sam needed him. The $7,750 a week he was then making was sacrificed for $50 a month. The expensive, endless, lavish wardrobe was tucked away in favor of olive drab. And most important, the lonely, melancholy existence at Encino ranch house was over; the constant reminders of Carole and their life together would be left behind. Gable had cherished these reminders. He had carefully preserved an old and battered table that he and Carole, in wild moments of hilarity, used to pound and chip and scar to give it a look of authentic antiquity—they would bang it with chains, scorch it with their lighted cigarets, scratch it with coins and keys.

Clark had literally turned Carole's bedroom into a shrine. After his return to the ranch house following Carole's death, Gable had simply closed the bedroom door, leaving it exactly as Carole had left it when she went to war. Nothing was touched. Even a small pile of face powder that Carole had spilled on the dresser remained as it was. And at nights, when the poignant memories of his beloved Carole overwhelmed him, Gable would quietly enter the darkness and stand there, feeling her presence . . . remembering. . . .

Now he was leaving it all behind.

Shortly after Clark enlisted, he was shipped, along with his old friend and cameraman, Andrew J. McIntyre, to the Officer's Candidate School in Miami, Florida, to begin a gruelling three-month training course. Off went the famous mustache and, within a month, in went the beltline as Clark, up at 5 A.M. and working in the broiling sun, sweated himself down from 195 to 185 pounds.

He emerged a second lieutenant upon his graduation from the Miami Officer's School, was upgraded to first looie after completing a gunnery course at Tyndall Field, Florida, and was upped to captain in the spring of 1943, while stationed at what for security purposes was always referred to as simply a "United States Bomber Station in England."

Gable's job in the Army Air Forces was to supervise the aerial photography on American bombing missions over enemy territory, make training films for use back in the States, study flying conditions and, at weaponry, train recruits in aerial gunnery.

Clark's first taste of action came on May 4, 1943, when he participated in a heavy American raid on the factory areas of Nazi-held Antwerp, Belgium.

He had gone along to shoot movies of the raid and managed to get several hundred feet of film. But he ended up shooting something else, too—a red-hot .50-caliber gun in the B-17's radio compartment.

"Here they come and here they go," Gable yelled as he blasted away at the attacking Focke-Wulffs that screamed through the skies at the raiding American Flying Fortress.

Clark unloosed several rounds at the German fighters, and while he probably scored several hits, he downed none of them. The "Eight Ball" itself was hit by enemy flak and one of the German fighters sent a 20-mm. shell through its nose. No one, fortunately, was injured.

Gable was overseas for seven months, and during that time he participated in five attacks over enemy territory. On each mission, he wore a silver chain around his neck. Dangling from the chain was a tiny box. And inside the box were the two jeweled ear clips that Carole Lombard had been wearing at the time of her death.

As might be expected, wherever Gable went, the girls were sure to go, and it was no different in England. During his stay there, he only made one foray into London because of the mobs that were sure to thrust themselves at him. Even in the tiny village near the base where Clark would frequently go with some of his comrades for a few evening beers, the girls would mob him. Once, he had to seek refuge in a church when some of his more ardent admirers ripped the buttons from his tunic. It got to the point, actually, where farmers were complaining to their local authorities that they couldn't hire any local "land girls" because they were forever hanging around the air base's gates hoping for a glimpse of their dashing hero.

After seven months in England, Gable returned to Hollywood—still as an Air Forces officer—and started editing some 50,000 feet of training film he had shot or directed overseas for an AAF training film "so the kids will know what it's like before they go over."

In an interview with one Hollywood reporter, Gable admitted that real-life airmen carrying out bombing missions over Nazi Europe didn't behave quite the way they did in the movie versions.

"They're very quiet," he said. "They know they have a good chance of coming back, but they also know there's the other chance they won't."

He said his most exciting flight was over "Happy Valley—the Ruhr."

"I don't know why the kids"—Gable was then 42, remember—"call it Happy Valley. Maybe it's because there are always so many Nazi fighters to meet you and you never get lonely. Our ship got a hit. She had about fifteen or eighteen flak holes, but nobody got hurt."

Andrew McIntyre, Gable's friend and cameraman who went along on the Ruhr raid, added his own postscript:

"We were lucky to get back."

At war's end, Gable was discharged as a major and wore on his chest the coveted Air Medal.

As everything else he undertook, his wartime performance was solid. He wanted and received little fanfare. It was a grim business fighting a war, and Gable gave it everything he had, but so did millions of others and Gable, wanting no special accolades, rebuked all attempts by others to glorify him.

Nevertheless he did achieve a rather special distinction.

According to Lieutenant General Ira Eaker, U. S. commanding officer during the air raids, German Air Minister Hermann Goering had announced a preferred roster of American Air Force officers he wanted taken dead or alive.

Colonel Hubert Zemke and Lieutenant Colonel Francis Gabreski, two of America's best fighter pilot aces with twenty-eight enemy aircraft each to their credit, were on the list, and so was a certain Captain Clark Gable.

Goering offered a $5,000 bonus, a furlough, and an immediate promotion to whoever downed the captain.

Both Zemke and Gabreski were shot down over Germany in 1944. Of the three, only Clark Gable survived the terrible war.

It had changed him, as war changes all men to some degree. It had taught him death and cruelty. And the war did something else to Clark Gable.

It aged him.

And in youth-oriented Hollywood, even the beginnings of age can be lethal.

# 14

## *Over So Soon?*

THE TROUBLE BEGAN WHEN the tall, graying bear of a man walking onto the Metro-Goldwyn-Mayer lot on that first visit was ex-Army Major Clark Gable, not Rhett Butler.

When the big studio brass, the inner circle of moviedom's hugest studio, poured out to meet him, they were welcoming home the dashing, smiling, devil-may-care of the incomparable *Gone With the Wind*, the last picture they and everyone else remembered him in.

Or so they thought. Maybe the vision of dollar signs dancing before their eyes clouded their perception, or maybe they simply refused to take a good look, but their biggest box office draw of all time wasn't the youngish Rhett Butler any more, he was a war-hardened man of 43, a little grimmer, a little grayer and only inches away from middle age.

In no time at all, the horror dawned on Gable that the bigwigs held the illusion that his youth would last forever. Even his old friend at MGM, Eddie Mannix, wanted Clark to remain young.

But Gable knew better. The first harsh breath of autumn was on him and he could feel its chill thrust in his bones and in his spirit.

Inevitably, they collided—Gable and the brass. They kept offering him the kind of roles he had handled so well in the 1930's. Gable kept shaking his head. It was a new decade and despite their plaintive hopes, time had not stood still for him.

For months, the battle raged, quietly but fiercely. In time, of course, they did settle on a film, and then another and then another and another, but each seemed more a desperate attempt to give Gable some sort of screen identity rather than provide him with a solid vehicle in which he could project the screen magic he had always possessed. The films were neither fish nor fowl. Gable knew it, the studio knew, and most important, the public knew it. They drew immense box offices, of course. The name Clark Gable on a movie marquee guaranteed a financial success. It always had. But the commodity the public automatically associated and equated with Gable was missing—a thing called quality.

His very first film, for example, was a farcical nonentity called *Adventure,* co-starring Greer Garson.

The MGM drumbeaters, ballyhooing Gable's return to the movies after the war, dished out the slogan "Gable's Back and Garson's Got Him." Although it grossed $5,000,000 as his loyal fans flocked to the nation's movie houses, it wasn't long before the chant was changed to "Gable's Back and Garson's Got Him—and You Can Have Them."

As disaster followed disaster, Clark became gloomy and uncertain of himself.

He felt his career as an actor was over. And since it was his life as well as his love, he thought that he himself, as a man, was through, too. Sullenly, he stayed away from the studio in the increasingly long lapses between pictures. More and more he withdrew into himself and for a brief while, so said the rumors at the time—he began to hit the bourbon bottle with a regularity that brought distress and even tears to his friends.

Then he reversed himself completely. He began dropping in with startling frequency at the gayer nightspots—places he and Carole Lombard would have avoided like the plague. He began snapping at co-workers at the studio, a thing he'd never done before.

In time, of course, Gable's great dignity brought his life back into proper perspective, but he remained essentially unhappy.

In the mid-50's, things had reached such an impasse that MGM and Gable parted company, ending one of the most successful relationships in Hollywood's history. It wasn't a particularly friendly break. Once, shortly after Gable had left and was working on the 20th Century-Fox lot as a free-lance actor, he nodded his head at the make-up man working on him and said grimly to a friend, "He's the only thing I wanted when I left MGM."

And at a party tossed in his honor on the eve of his leaving MGM, Clark, ignoring all the MGM brass gathered around him, stood and proposed a toast "to my friends and associates who are no longer alive."

As always, when Gable's imminent departure was announced, the rumor mills began to grind out their chaff. Most of them reported that it was because of a personality rift with this executive or that. But Gable himself put the record straight.

"It was simply that long succession of bad pictures," he said.

With his departure from MGM, Gable perked up noticeably. He was happy to be picking his own scripts, choosing his own director, selecting his own staff.

Nevertheless, it wasn't until 1955 that he seemed absolutely satisfied with a post-war film.

The movie was *Mogambo*, a re-make of *Red Dust* in which Jean Harlow and Mary Astor had co-starred with him twenty-one years before. In the newer version, Ava Gardner had the Harlow role and twenty-six-year-old Grace Kelley was cast in the Astor part.

*Mogambo* was an immediate success—both commercially and, in the opinion of most reviewers, artistically. And it hadn't been out very long when MGM belatedly concluded it might have been making a mistake with Gable during those previous ten years. The King hadn't changed, only the terrible picture material they'd been giving him.

One of Gable's friends later told reporters that "Clark was offered everything but the MGM sink to come back, even to sharing the profits, something that MGM had never before offered. Eddie Mannix, Clark's old friend, was sent over to London to win him back, but it was too late. The damage had been done."

The tide turned with *Mogambo*. Soon the Gable whom millions of Americans had adored and respected, was back in his proper niche. His pictures were good. Some were great. And as the years went by, they became even better.

By 1957, when Clark did *Teacher's Pet* with Doris Day, Gable's fans saw some of the deft comedy touch he had shown of old, the same sparkling kind of performance that had won him an Oscar for *It Happened One Night*.

From the point of view of his career, Gable's battle was over. He'd fought and he'd won.

But going back to 1949, Clark was waging another battle,

a far more important one—the dark, despairing struggle against loneliness. Actually, the battle had begun a few years earlier, but he found himself unable to make headway. In one respect, Clark had miscalculated. Taunted and annoyed by the loneliness that surrounded him, hoping for and seeking a way to rid himself of the feeling, and terribly anxious to find companionship—Clark Gable went in pursuit of a mirage.

He began to look for another Carole Lombard . . .

# 15

## *Marriage to Lady Ashley—a Brief Storm*

IF A HISTORICAL SURVEY WERE to be made of the greatest sirens through the ages, there's little doubt that Sylvia, Lady Stanley would be well up in the vanguard, for rarely has there been a woman with a more dazzling record of male conquests. The Greeks and Trojans fought a war over Helen; Marc Antony was so bewitched by Cleopatra that he defied the power of Rome, and DuBarry and Pompadour made toys of two kings of France.

But none of them can put their records alongside the magnificent accomplishments in the marital olympics of this slim Englishwoman born Sylvia Edith Louise Hawkes. She was married to two of Great Britain's noblest peers and one of Hollywood's first great kings, Douglas Fairbanks, of the silent screen, before she became acquainted with another king—Clark Gable.

Sylvia's saga in the whirlpool of life began roughly in 1910 in the cockney East End of London. There is a vagueness over the exact year of her birth as there is about her family background. Some reports say her father was a footman, others persist he was a London pubkeeper. But footman or pubkeeper or whatever—humble birth and humble surroundings have not stood as obstacles for those born to be famous. And Sylvia was one of those who was.

When she was but a girl of fifteen, Sylvia's beauty had already begun to flower, and her golden hair, baby blue eyes, delicately chiseled features, and willowy figure projected an image of rare and refined womanhood. We are now probably in the early 1920s and we see Sylvia as a fashionable model in the employ of a London silk lingerie firm. Across the Atlantic, Clark Gable is still a struggling young lumberjack and part-time actor, and he has not yet shaken the corn from behind his big ears.

Like Clark Gable, who was determined to make something of himself as an actor, Sylvia was infused with a will to achieve for herself a prominence in life. As a model of filmy underthings for prospective buyers, Sylvia had acquired the nickname of "Silky" and it was not to her liking. She soon tired of being ogled in dainty attire and decided to move up in the world. She became a chorus girl.

While dancing in the Winter Garden—where ogling was even more in vogue—Sylvia had one of those rare opportunities that come to a chorus girl. She was introduced to Anthony, Lord Ashley, one of England's most eligible bachelors, son of the Earl of Shaftesbury and the Countess Lady of the Bedchamber of Queen Mary. They were married on February 3, 1927.

But the marriage lasted only about a year, after which Sylvia left her lord and returned to her theatrical friends. There followed a period of great embarrassment for his lordship when his wife's name became linked romantically with that of millionaire Sir Henry Birkin and to Lord Beaverbrook. Lord Ashley inserted ads in London newspapers announcing he was no longer responsible for his wife's debts.

But his lordship did not consider divorce until 1934—when he named Douglas Fairbanks as co-respondent. This, however, did not happen until after Sylvia had a brief interlude of romances with Michael Farmer, the ex-husband of Gloria Swanson, and with Sir Robert Throckmorton. When the divorce became final, Lady Ashley became Mrs. Douglas Fairbanks. The marriage took place in Paris in March, 1936. At this very moment in Hollywood, Clark Gable was enjoying bachelor status again after his separation from Rhea Langham—and was dating Carole Lombard.

Fairbanks, who had earlier been married to Mary Pickford, the sweetheart of silent films, was now no longer a star; his son Douglas Fairbanks Jr. was trying to carry on in the tradition of his father, but Douglas Sr. was not the toast of the film capital that he had once held under his spell. Fairbanks brought his charming bride to Hollywood and immediately she captured the town with her gracious, aristocratic ways. The marriage seemed to be a success and it went along in clover until the king of the silent flickers died in December, 1939, leaving his "beloved wife" $1,000,000. Sylvia was now not only beautiful and famous, but wealthy as well.

The rest came easy—she had her pick of practically any man she wanted. In New York, among others, there was Barbara Hutton's cousin, millionaire Woolworth Donahue, who panted for Sylvia like a hound after the fox. But considerable indecision beset Sylvia before she finally made her move. It was in the direction of another titled aristocrat of English stock—handsome, dark-haired Edward John Stanley, sixth Baron of Alderly.

Lord Stanley married Sylvia in Boston on January 18, 1944. Songwriter Cole Porter gave the bride away but even his melodic influence could not drown out the sour notes that Sylvia and Lord Stanley soon struck in their household. By the following September they were separated. On June 15, 1948, following a twenty-minute hearing, Lord Stanley was granted a divorce from Sylvia on grounds of desertion.

This launched Lady Ashley, as she persisted in calling herself, into an orbit of social dating with a host of eligible men of two continents. But none seemed to suit her. Her travels took her back to Hollywood. She was now about 42 and unquestionably more beautiful than ever. She was charming, polished, gay, and totally self-assured in the lofty precincts of international cafe society, and beyond all that her likeness to Carole Lombard was startling.

And her baby blue eyes all at once became fixed on one tall, oaken hunk of man. He was another king—the King of the talkies.

He was Clark Gable.

At the moment, Clark Gable appeared to the world to still be mourning the death of Carole Lombard and marriage seemed like the furthest thing from his mind. Friends thought Clark was pursuing a mirage, searching for something of Carole in all of his post-war romances with many of Hollywood's great beauties. For the record, here is but a brief list of the damsels whom Clark dated during the period:

Marilyn Maxwell, Paulette Goddard, Iris Bynum, Anita Colby, Virginia Grey, Elaine White, Audrey Totter, Joan Harrison, and the fabulous, sophisticated grandmother, Dolly O'Brien.

But destiny had decreed that Clark and Sylvia meet. Their get-together was quite by accident—they met at a dinner party in Hollywood agent Charles Feldman's house. They were formally introduced by, of all people, agent Minna Wallis —remember Minna, who sold Irving Thalberg on Gable?

The date was Saturday, December 17, 1949.

Early that afternoon, Minna Wallis met Sylvia at Romanoff's for lunch. Minna and Sylvia were the best of friends, and their talk was about the party at Feldman's house that night—and about Clark Gable, who was to be Sylvia's date. Clark and Sylvia had seen each other around, but never dated. This was to be their first.

Sylvia had spent most of that day shopping in crowded stores for dolls she wanted to buy for the children of some friends as Christmas presents. The ordeal had taken quite a bit out of Sylvia, so Minna suggested:

"Why don't you come to my house? You can freshen up with some of my electrical equipment."

It would go without saying that any gal who had a date with Clark Gable would spend a week getting ready for it. Not Sylvia.

"No, thank you, Minna," she said, "I'll go home to the beach house"—the one she inherited from Douglas Fairbanks —"and I'll just have time to change. I suppose I should really wear something nice."

Without taking too much trouble, Sylvia showed up at the party as its most stunning guest. Gable's eyes lit up at the sight of the shapely, blonde, blue-eyed creature who at once reminded him of someone from the long-ago—Carole Lombard.

Right then and there Clark made up his mind he was going to marry Sylvia. But the Feldman house wasn't the place to ask a lady for her hand. Clark decided to wait.

He waited until 2:30 o'clock in the morning when he took Sylvia by the hand and escorted her to his Cadillac, to drive her home. They were alone in the car now and they were alone with their thoughts. They were, really, two very lonely people. Christmas and the New Year always make people who are lonely more sensitive, more aware of their dreariness. Clark and Sylvia had both dreaded the holidays—but Clark dreaded them even more than Sylvia. . . .

This was the right psychological moment for a proposal of marriage, this moment in the Cadillac, which had all at once come to an abrupt and unscheduled stop against a small concrete abutment.

"You'll have to excuse my lousy driving," Clark apologized to Sylvia as he got out to survey the damage to the right front fender. "You see," Clark joked, "I'm not used to driving so slowly." Clark wasn't kidding either, because back home in the garage he had a little streak of greased lightning called a Jaguar—like Sylvia, a British importation—which could blast off to 130-mile-per-hour speeds; and Gable was always trying to better the 45-minute driving time between his Encino ranch and the studio.

Well, there they were, Clark and Sylvia, enjoying a good laugh over the accident. Clark had laughed like this before, but it was so long ago. But the situation then wasn't much different than now—only then it was with Carole. It happened often. Clark, the restless type, would awaken Carole at two or three in the morning and say, "Let's go for a drive." And Carole would always say, "Okay, Pappy." And off they would go. Once in a while, too, Clark would have a mishap with the car and he and Carole would have a good laugh over it, just as he and Sylvia were laughing now.

# CLARK GABLE
## His Movie Life
## His Leading Ladies

Clark Gable and Jean Harlow

One of Clark's first leading ladies was "the Blonde Bombshell," Jean Harlow. Their sizzling love scenes made early movie-screen history!

Clark's bit role as a gambler in **A Free Soul** called for him to haul off and slap Norma Shearer's aristocratic face. It made him a star!

The famous Gable-Harlow rain barrel scene from **Red Dust,** 1932.

The next big star to snag Gable as a leading man was Joan Crawford. His bit role with her in **Dance, Fools, Dance** (above) led to many co-starring movies. The public liked them together. Below, they're in **Strange Cargo.**

Clark Gable made love to all types of leading ladies: the great Garbo in **Susan Lennox** (above); madcap Carole Lombard in **No Man Of Her Own** (top right); singer Jeanette MacDonald in **San Francisco** (right). But he proved he could score without a leading lady, too. **Mutiny On The Bounty** (below), was one of his top performances.

The "walls of Jericho" divided the motel room Clark shared with Claudette Colbert in **It Happened One Night,** which won the Academy Award in 1934.

Sophisticated Myrna Loy succumbed to Clark's charm as an aviation daredevil in **Test Pilot.**

Clark surprised everyone when he did a dance routine in 1939's **Idiot's Delight.**

One of his closest friends, Spencer Tracy, starred with him in several films. Here, they're in a scene from **Boom Town.**

**GONE WITH THE WIND**

No film ever created as much excitement or won as much acclaim as **Gone With The Wind.** The search for the feminine lead took three years, and English actress Vivien Leigh finally drew the prized role of Scarlett O'Hara. Clark Gable—nominated unanimously for the part of Rhett Butler — turned in a dashing performance that will never be forgotten. The pictures on these two pages are three of the dramatic highlights of the movie — Rhett proposing to Scarlett, the flight from Atlanta, and a passionate love scene in a field at Tara.

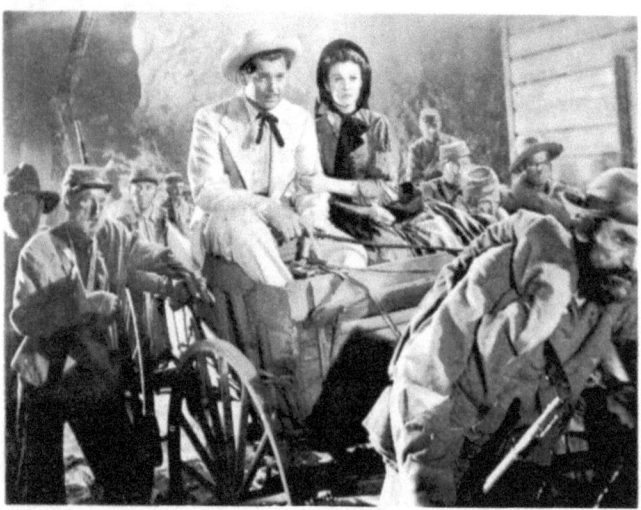

Clark and Lana Turner made a torrid combination in **Honky Tonk,** 1941.

122

In **Comrade X,** 1940, Gable played a newspaper reporter who falls in love with a Russian girl, Hedy Lamarr.

His first movie when he returned from World War II was **Adventure.** Remember the slogan, "Gable's back and Garson's got him"?

123

In 1953 **Red Dust,** was re-made under the name **Mo-gambo.** Clark again played the lead—and did the same scene (above) with Ava Gardner he'd done with Harlow 21 years before (page 114).

**Command Decision** (above) was a hit, even though it had no women in the cast. Two more post-war movies: **Band of Angels** with Yvonne DeCarlo (left) and **Key to the City,** Loretta Young (below).

Clark played romantic leading roles well
into his fifties. He won Doris Day away from
Gig Young in **Teacher's Pet,** 1958.

He loved his role in **But Not For Me,** with Lee J. Cobb
and Lilli Palmer. It kidded older men who romance
young girls!

A new generation of movie-goers thrilled to Clark in his later years, the daughters of the fans he had when he first started. Here, he plays opposite Italian star Sophia Loren in **It Started In Naples**, in 1960.

**His Last Movie
His Last Leading Lady**

The last in a long line of glamorous leading ladies was Marilyn Monroe. Clark Gable died shortly after they finished making **The Misfits.**

Suddenly Clark stopped laughing. Suddenly his face was masked in seriousness. Suddenly he looked into Sylvia's eyes. Suddenly he took her in his arms. And suddenly he said it: "Sylvia, let's get married."

And Sylvia, swept off her feet, surprised beyond her wildest dreams, overcome by the electric and pulsating charms that had driven millions of the world's women into ecstasy, couldn't resist the proposal.

The next day, Monday, December 20th, Clark phoned his best friend, Metro publicity boss Howard Strickling.

"What are you doing?" Clark wanted to know.

"I'm working," Howard said.

Clark laughed.

"You'd better stop working and come on over," he said. "I want to talk to you. I want to marry quietly."

"Then," Howard replied without being too overwhelmed by the news, "you'd better do it right away."

The next day, accompanied by Strickling, Clark and Sylvia drove off to the Alisal Ranch near Santa Barbara for the wedding. And, on Tuesday, December 21, 1949, the former Lady Sylvia Ashley, darling of the cafe set, glib conversationalist, and a superficial carbon copy of Carole Lombard, became Mrs. Sylvia Gable. Sylvia's voice trembled during the ceremony and her hand shook as she cut the cake with a sword. Later, Clark helped Sylvia wipe away the champagne she spilled as her hand continued to shake like a first-time bride.

The honeymoon was in Honolulu. It lasted two weeks. On January 16th, Clark brought his bride home to the ranch in Encino. Sylvia had been there only once before, the day she and Clark were married.

Sylvia almost at once found what she had expected. "Everywhere she looked," a friend related, "it seemed Sylvia was surrounded by Carole's presence. There was the long pine table in the dining room that Carole and Clark had so much fun making an 'antique,' scarring it with cigarettes and hammering it with chains; there was the Staffordshire china, the pewter drinking mugs, the pine and the maple—everything that reminded Gable of the wife he still loved, the ghost of Carole Lombard.

"So naturally, Sylvia had to change things, just as she was trying to change over Gable. She added a guest house, feminized the rooms, which Carole had kept as Clark liked them. Not long afterward, Sylvia took off for England to retrieve some of her antiques that were in storage."

It was a pretty thorough changeover—but it looked more like Mayfair than Encino.

Gable didn't seem to mind. He had given Sylvia a free hand and Clark never interfered—not until Sylvia tried to fire Clark's old houseman, Martin, a favorite of Carole's, and install an English butler. Then Clark put his foot down.

Gable, always a frugal figure despite the millions he had made, also couldn't tolerate Sylvia's free-spending ways.

"Clark just couldn't understand," the friend said, "why Sylvia needed a personal maid when she seemed quite capable of drawing her own bath. Clark also was beside himself over Sylvia's other extravagances. At first he went along with her, but as she continued to spend money like there was no tomorrow, Clark wanted her to put a stop to it."

Gable himself revealed later that in something like three weeks after the elopement he had discovered his mistake in marrying Sylvia. But it was a mistake he had to live with, for a while at least.

With Carole, Clark had a woman who subordinated every desire to her husband's—and was happy to do it. But Sylvia couldn't be happy unless Gable was living her way—the way she fancied a gentleman or country squire would live.

Clark also found he had lost the one cherished possession in life that seemed to give him the zest for living—his privacy. With Sylvia, Gable had none of it.

Sylvia loved people. And she loved her relatives—like her sister, Vera Bleck. Time and again, the stories go, Sylvia had Vera and her husband, Basil, with the children, Timothy, then seventeen, and Loretta, fourteen, come to stay at the Encino ranch. It annoyed Gable, who was once so disturbed that he had to say it:

"After I lost Carole, I didn't mix much. I liked my own home. I didn't like a family underfoot—not even my own.

"And while Sylvia's sister and her children didn't live much at the ranch, they were there a good deal of the time. A man's home is his castle, even though mine happens to be a rather simple ranch."

The proof of Clark's words can be found in his actions. Toward the end of his life, Clark's widowed father married again. Clark wanted him near him. He was his only blood relative. But, much as Clark adored his father, he bought him a separate house in Coldwater Canyon, below the Gable ranch in the San Fernando Valley. It was there the father lived. Clark would see his father often and their relationship was a sober and sincere one, not goppy and superficial.

Yet Sylvia seemed to brush aside Clark's wishes for seclusion—and it laid the groundwork for the unhappiness that was to follow.

Carole, of whom Sylvia reminded Gable so much, was always ready, willing, and able to pick up and go on a fishing and hunting trip with Clark. Sylvia tried, but it was a pathetic attempt.

One of the best examples was the time shortly after their marriage when Clark went on location for the making of

*Across the Wide Missouri.* Sylvia couldn't have been more uncomfortable if she had been parachuted into the deepest jungles of Africa. It was just too rough for her, this American Wild West type of existence. Sylvia, who had been used to camping out at Romanoff's and the Colony, decided to bring some of the comforts of home along.

She ordered an ice-box brought in to make cabin life more endurable and even had trees and shrubbery planted to improve on the scene that nature had neglected. The studio could see Sylvia was no outdoor gal by any stretch of the imagination, but it, nevertheless, decided to put out some publicity stills showing Mrs. Gable as a rugged camper roughing it on location. So they shot pictures of her cooking.

They neglected one detail that immediately removed the action from the realm of credibility—they forgot to remove the diamond sparklers from her fingers!

Six months after the marriage, despite the rumors sweeping the film capital that things were not going well at Encino, Sylvia was quoted by a well-known Hollywood columnist:

"We both have been married before, and we know it takes two to make a quarrel, and we are not going to make the mistakes either of us made in any previous marriage. Besides, we have so many things in common.

"I love to fish, and I love my home. There is only one thing we won't share together, and that's hunting. I'll go with him while he hunts, but I couldn't shoot a gun, nor could I kill anything."

But Clark's home and his recreation weren't the only things Sylvia tried to change. Gable himself was on her agenda. And during his marriage Sylvia constantly reminded him that she had certain ideas on what a gentleman should be like, a quality she thought Clark should even carry into his pictures. Actually she managed to accomplish this in one of his films, ironically enough entitled *To Please a Lady*.

The script, dealing with the story about an Indianapolis Speedway driver, had to be practically rewritten to overcome Sylvia's objections to Clark being cast as a drunken bum.

She insisted he establish his gentlemanliness by donning a tuxedo in the picture!

It amused Gable's friends to no end that Sylvia, a former chorus girl who became a lady by marriage, tried to make a "gentleman" of a man like Gable—the Clark Gable who was celebrated for his born qualities of courtesy, kindness, and gentlemanliness.

This was one of the reasons, just one of the many reasons that Clark resolved that his marriage to Sylvia had to end— and that, when it was over, he would never marry again. He had had it.

The breakup came just after Clark and Sylvia had celebrated their paper anniversary. It was in March, 1951, when Sylvia filed for divorce, retaining noted Hollywood attorney Jerry Giesler. Many reasons were offered to explain the breakup, but the most popular version of the day—which was adduced from the divorcing parties—was that they each were hard to get along with.

It must have come as quite a shock to the columnist who had only recently interviewed Sylvia about her happy home life with Clark. The columnist went way out on a limb after her talk with Mrs. Gable, saying:

"I have always been very fond of both Clark and Sylvia, and I look to see them celebrate their golden wedding anniversary."

Well, it wasn't a bad guess—just missed it by forty-nine years.

Incidentally, this was the same columnist who scooped the world by breaking the news that Jean Arthur was going to play Scarlett O'Hara.

On October 4th, Clark himself filed a separate divorce suit in Reno, after he and Sylvia couldn't agree on a property settlement. Sylvia, according to the most persistent Hollywood rumor, was determined to walk away from the marriage with a million dollars. Gable was just as determined not to give Sylvia a cent, maintaining she had spent more than he had earned during their marriage—and he was earning more than half a million a year then.

To foil Sylvia's attempt to nick him for California alimony, Clark quietly moved with his fortune to Nevada, bag, baggage, and all. He even ordered the sprawling Encino ranch sold and bought a 3,000-acre ranch near Reno. Clark also moved most of his personal belongings to Glerock, Nevada, took out a Nevada auto license, paid the Nevada poll tax to qualify as a citizen, and transferred sizable accounts to Reno and Carbon City banks. He even switched his membership in the Shriners from Los Angeles to Reno.

But Sylvia obtained an injunction almost immediately in Santa Monica Superior Court, which ordered Gable to show cause why he should not be restrained from getting a Nevada decree. It was a strategic move on Sylvia's part. Sylvia was gambling on the likelihood that she'd have a better chance for a property settlement if she won her own California decree first.

Sylvia finally was granted her wish in April, 1952. An eleven-page property settlement gave her a large but unspecified sum and a lien of ten per cent on Gable's income for a year—about $75,000.

Once again Sylvia became Lady Ashley, still a winner in the

realm of high finance, still a loser in the deeper realm of the heart.

And Gable was free—free from the mistake that might have changed his entire career.

# 16

## *Second Wind*

AFTER HIS DIVORCE FROM Lady Ashley, Clark Gable resolved never to marry again. But a man's resolve is vulnerable to influences, especially when those influences are concentrated in an extraordinarily beautiful woman with a wealth of personal charm, tremendous gaiety and enormous sense of life about her. And more so when those influences include, additionally, a bright, sharp, intelligent mind combined with a patrician loveliness and magnificent natural blonde hair, clear blue eyes that reflect the cerulean sky, and flawless, lovely white skin that rivals the driven snow. Moreover, when those influences also constitute a gorgeous figure—well, it's mighty hard for a man to resist.

Even if the man was Clark Gable, the movie idol of every woman from sixteen to sixty.

The explanation is simple enough, for not every woman from sixteen to sixty could match the exquisite charm and beauty and personality of the *one* woman who proved to all Hollywood, to all the world, that those who bet against Clark marrying again were dead wrong. That woman was Kathleen Williams Spreckels, and there is a story about her.

Kathleen Williams, or Kay, as she is called, was not a woman who entered Clark Gable's life for the first time after he fell away from Sylvia, but was an old, old acquaintance—dating back to the wartime year of 1943 when she first denied she was going to marry him. Actually they had known each other to say hello to since 1942.

Kay was one of the many Hollywood girls who had gone out—and fallen in love—with Clark Gable, and rumors that she and the King were to be married were bandied about along with the gossip about Clark's matrimonial intentions with Loretta Young, and Mary Taylor, and the string of other girls whom Clark had dated.

In those days, Kay was on the threshold of a promising movie career. Already behind her were two marriages and a highly successful modeling career.

She had begun life on August 7, 1916, in Erie, Pa., as Kay Williams, and after a rather uneventful childhood she grew into a beautiful teenager who was briefly married to a young but penurious engineer, Parker Capps. Then she came to New York. She was twenty then and she literally took the city by storm as she stepped into the world of modeling. By 1940 she was being hailed as a combination of Lillian Russell, Maxine Elliott, and Anna Held. The Authors and Artists Convention chose her then as the most beautiful model of the year.

When she went to the Palm Beach Biltmore, four hundred women lined up in the lobby and on the terrace to see her—that's how beautiful she was. It was inevitable, then, that Hollywood would beckon. And when she was proffered a movie contract, Kay signed and was off to join the Metro-Goldwyn-Mayer stable of starlets.

But being a $75-a-week starlet was not Kay's cup of tea. Especially not after the $75 an hour she earned in modeling. So on November 25, 1942, she married Martin deAlzaga Unzue, a multi-millionaire. Around the cocktail circuit in this country, deAlzaga Unzue was better known as "Macoco." He had previously been wed to the socialite daughter of the Moncure Robinsons of Philadelphia and then to swingy Kathryn Ray, the "Pendulum Girl" in an Earl Carroll theatrical show which the late Mayor Hylan of New York had threatened to close because Kathryn had shown so much of her ample charms.

When Macoco swung over and took Kay for his wife, the marriage lasted ten days. Then Macoco sued for annulment on the ground that Kay was a wife in name only. He dropped the suit later but after eight months Kay herself sued on grounds of cruelty and asked for $750 alimony. She charged that Macoco "flew into jealous rages" when any other man paid attention to her. It was in her application for her final papers in the divorce that Kay denied she was going to marry Clark Gable.

And all rumors of such a possibility abruptly ended in 1945 when Kay became the fifth wife of multi-millionaire sugar heir Adolph P. Spreckels.

Kay's marriage to the sugar king was far from being sweet. But they held the bonds of matrimony intact through the birth of two children, Adolph 3rd, born in 1949, and Joan, born in 1951. Then the marriage soured and Kay sued for divorce. This was in 1952—the same year Clark Gable won his freedom from Lady Ashley.

It came as quite a jolt to the readers of the morning and afternoon papers across the country to learn that Clark Gable was in Kay Spreckels' divorce suit, dragged in by Adolph who complained that things came to a pretty pass when his wife invited Clark out to see the bougainvillaea.

Just to make things clear, the bougainvillaea is a genus of ornamental tropical American woody vines with brilliant red or purple floral bracts. Spreckels had one such species growing near the swimming pool of his luxurious Beverly Hills home.

When Spreckels testified in court, he unraveled a saga that rivaled the scenario of a Gable movie. Spreckels said he was sick one night and Kay had gone to a party at the Jack Bennys'. Kay was escorted home by Gable and Mr. and Mrs. Walter Lang. When they reached home, Spreckels went on, he didn't like what went on. From his sick bed, he swore, he could hear Kay calling to Gable to come down and look at the bougainvillaea. Because it was some distance from the house, Spreckels was concerned.

He was relieved when Gable wouldn't go—not even after Kay had called to him several times. When she came into his room later, Spreckels said, he told Kay he didn't think she should have asked Gable to see the bougainvillaea—at least not with the inviting tone of voice Adolph thought he had heard.

"She told me it was nothing," Spreckels testified, "she already had had an affair with Gable."

Kay promptly denied this and sailed in with her own rebuttal—that Spreckels was impossible to live with because of his violent temper. He was, she swore, always raising cane.

Kay's statement fell as mere words upon the court, but in December of 1953 her claim about Adolph's temper became grim reality.

In the interim Kay had won her suit and gotten custody of the children as well as $6,000 a year for twelve years and $600 a month for support of Adolph 3rd and Joan. She had asked for $3,000 a month alimony and half the community property.

Now on this December day, the children were staying with their father and Kay had gone to Spreckels' house to visit them. Things came to a violent head when Kay had Adolph arrested, charging he punched, her, knocked her down, kicked her, and beat her on the head with her own slipper. In his defense, Spreckels said Kay had been drinking and threw a vase at him. Kay said she had only two belts of liquor compared with the innumerable belts rained on her by Spreckels—and she disputed any doubts about her state of sobriety by quoting Adolph as saying:

"I'll fix that pretty face of yours . . ."

The court was convinced. Spreckels was sentenced to thirty days in jail.

The marriage was washed up and Kay made no cryptic statements this time about not marrying Clark Gable as she had done when she had shed her Argentine. Only Spreckels' one statement was left to haunt Kay as she went off with her children to live in a $75,000 home in Beverly Hills that Adolph had given her during the marriage.

"Kay once told me," Spreckels said in Los Angeles Superior Court, shaking his head sadly, " 'only money makes my passion burn.' "

An expert who searched out the finer details of the agreement with Adolph, said he found that besides the alimony, the child support, and the $75,000 house, Kay also received during the marriage $20,000 worth of furnishings for the home, plus furs, jewelry, stocks, bonds, and two trust funds. All added up, the expert said, Kay came out with about $501,947—plus her lawyers' fees.

With Kay and Clark both free from their respective spouses, Hollywood wisenheimers were quick to predict that the sparks of friendship struck up near the bougainvillaea might well be rekindled into a raging fire of romance.

The first sparks, actually, didn't flare up near the bougainvillaea but many years before, in 1942, when Clark was introduced to Kay Williams by MGM executive Benny Thau. Kay fell in love with Clark Gable at first sight!

But falling in love with Gable at first glimpse wasn't any distinction—it put Kay in very good company. Every woman who met Gable fell in love with him.

The time of their first meeting was shortly after Carole Lombard's death. Clark was immediately struck by Kay's vivaciousness, flawless figure, precise grooming, and striking resemblance to Carole. She was definitely his type. Kay was twenty-five years old then, a girl of sparkle, a girl of fun, a girl who kept the fact that she was a divorcée a deep, dark secret. Clark began to see her. Just a bit, because he also was seeing a bit of several other girls, too—also blondes, like Virginia Grey, for one.

But Kay got more of Clark's attention than the others. He even took Kay down to the ranch, which was the supreme moment in any girl's life. Doves were cooing all over the place —they were the hundreds of descendants of the seven doves that Carole had sent Clark after their first fight, and the many others that came during subsequent quarrels. All through the years that followed, the doves stayed and kept multiplying. Clark was very sentimental about these birds, so much so that he never allowed one to be killed.

Since Gable had paid her the supreme compliment by bringing her to Encino, Kay decided she wanted to marry him. She wanted him almost desperately. Then she did what many a girl has done, not only with Gable, but with average guys all over the world. She got pushy—and possessive.

What followed was a characteristic Gable defensive maneuver in cases of pushy, possessive women. He took Kay home one night after a very pleasant evening out, kissed her good-night—and walked straight out of her life for ten solid years. What Kay did also was characteristic of the actions of most girls who had seen the last of Clark Gable—she married her Argentine moneybags.

Now, after all the long years, Clark and Kay met again. It happened at the Jack Bennys—the night that the boungainvillaea incident took place. That night Clark found a Kay Williams far different than the Kay Williams he had known —she was older, wiser, a mother, and had the good sense to conceal the fact that she was still in love with him, although married to Spreckels.

It was after that incident, after Spreckels got the episode headlined in the papers, that Clark called up Kay for the first time.

"Are you all right?" he asked.

"Oh, sure," Kay replied. She waited.

"Your children are all right, too?" he put in.

"Just fine," she answered. "I don't think there's any cause for alarm."

"I'd like to see your kids sometime," Clark said.

"Any time."

"I'll call you."

A week went by. Clark didn't call. But, instead, he went over to Kay's house on a surprise visit and met Adolph and Joan. A few days later Clark suggested that the kids might like to visit the ranch. Kay thought that was a wonderful idea.

When Kay visited the ranch with the children, Clark discovered that she had changed. She had learned to cook. And she had learned to shoot. Very soon, they were off hunting and fishing together—and more importantly, they were laughing together.

To the outside world, there were no visible smoke signals that came from the raging fires of love, although there were a few puffs of smoke here and there to start the rumor factories working again on a new Gable romance. But the dates Clark and Kay had were interrupted by long separations as Gable traipsed off to Europe, the Far East, to Africa, and Mexico on film-making expeditions or vacation and hunting trips.

Gable himself never would comment about any romantic interest in Kathleen, as he called her. As for Kay, it was the same extremity of silence. Those who knew Kay intimately knew something that the rest of the world did not know—that aside from her extraordinary beauty and personal charm, Kay possessed an innate understanding of men and an uncanny ability to sense their likes and dislikes. Moreover, she had learned the lesson that few women learn—to keep the mouth shut. She had learned it the hard way and suffered for it for all those years when Gable would have nothing to do with her.

Other women learned the hard way, too.

For example: When, in 1953, Gable went to Europe, he took up briefly with the beauteous Turkish-born French model Suzanne Dadolle. The couple were billed as more than an "item"—theirs was called a "blazing romance." But Suzanne let Gable slip off the marriage hook by letting it get around that she and Clark were engaged. Clark took the next train out of Paris and never returned.

"Marriage talk," a man who knew Gable well observed after the Suzanne thing ended, "was enough to ruin many of Clark's beautiful friendships, though he had been known to have a change of heart overnight, as he did with Silkie Ashley. But in Suzanne's case, it was different. When she let slip that Clark proposed, the honeymoon was over."

Kay knew Clark's skittishness about talk of marriage, so she never engaged in it. When reporters asked her how did she see things in Paris—meaning was she worried about Suzanne stealing Clark's heart—all that Kay would say was:

"Do you mean Paris, Kentucky?"

When Clark had gone off earlier, in 1952, to Africa with Ava Gardner and a relative newcomer on the Hollywood scene named Grace Kelly to make *Mogambo*, reporters tried to sensationalize a romance between Clark and Grace. In the picture, Grace vied with Ava for hunter Clark Gable's romantic attentions. It was natural for the rumor mongers to turn it into an "item."

Actually, few persons were capable of understanding Gable's true motives in any off-screen relationship with a beautiful, younger woman, even if the girl herself might have entertained different notions. Clark was for an actual fact acting simply and purely with Big Brother interests.

For example, when Gable chose lynx-eyed Ava for the part in *Mogambo* played by Jean Harlow in the earlier film version that was *Red Dust,* not a few people felt that there might have been something between them. That was not so, however. Ava, who jeopardized her marriage to Frank Sinatra by journeying to Africa and missing the Christmas holidays at home, did it for only one reason—the furtherance of her professional career. Ava was grateful to the Great Gable for the chance he had given her in *The Hucksters* and for tutoring her in *Show Boat*—a film in which he didn't even appear—that she could not turn down the offer.

"He was the first man," Ava said, "to give me confidence on the set."

In Africa, Clark deliberately shied away from Miss Kelly, for the very reason that he knew what the columnists would make of it if he were seen with her off the set. But toward the end of the film, Clark decided to ignore the gossips and took Grace into the African brush for some serious hunting.

That gave the grapevine new fodder. And when Gable and Grace began to sit alone in the location mess tent, it lent new impetus to the rumors. But Grace had a logical explanation:

"That was only during the time Frank Sinatra visited Ava. The rest of the time we three—Ava, Clark, and I—ate together. We're just good friends . . ."

That should have stopped it but the talk went on. Gable was responsible for the next resumption of romantic gossip, for when he came home to Hollywood he bragged all over the lot what a great trouper Grace was, describing in detail how she had pushed through the brush, got scratched, fell, and never complained. His admiration was misinterpreted as love.

"It was almost as though he were talking about Carole," an intimate said, "but the age disparity was too great—twenty-eight years."

In her good time, Grace Kelly, who was a mere twenty-four then, commented about the suggested May-December romance when finally some reporter told Grace she was seen to break down and cry in London when saying goodbye to Clark.

"If I cried," said the tall, lovely blonde, "and I don't remember doing so, it was probably over the fact that I had to leave all that beautiful Georgian silver behind in customs." Then as if she feared her remark might be considered disparaging, she hastened to add:

"Perhaps it might have been different if it weren't for the difference in ages."

And do we have a statement from Kay about this episode?

Yes, Kay did have something to say when asked—while Clark was still in Africa—what she thought of the climate over there on the Dark Continent, did she think it was pretty hot?

"I suppose so," Kay smiled, "the geography says it is."

Incidentally, Clark's years'-long dream of going big game hunting had been fulfilled on his trip to Africa. Because everyone knew he was a crack shot, he was asked to furnish game for the porters and other native workers.

How did Gable like shooting big game? He didn't!

"Big game hunting in Africa is organized slaughter of fine animals," he commented. "If I go back, it will be with a camera."

Once again the Grace Kelly rumors floated through the film capital when the King asked for her as his co-star in *Soldier of Fortune*, but the talk died quickly when Miss Kelly was obliged to turn it down because of another commitment.

In her place, Susan Hayward—one of 20th Century-Fox's

biggest money makers—was recommended. Gable looked puzzled for a moment.

"Susan Hayward?" he frowned. "Who is she?"

The roar of laughter could be heard clear down to Hollywood and Vine. Could it be that Gable, who was the ruling monarch of the film capital, did not know one of the first ladies of the castle? Actually, Clark had drawn a blind spot. And amid the roars of laughter, he sensed his faux pas.

"Okay, okay," he grinned, "I goofed. I've known right along she's a big star, and I've known it for years—but it's just one of those things. The name didn't click for a second. After all, you know I never go to the movies."

When Gable left for Hong Kong to make *Soldier of Fortune*, Kay again stayed home in Bel-Air—remember, she had two young children and probably couldn't have made the trip even if she had wanted. But if she had wanted—that might have scared Clark away. Like Penelope, knitting all day and unraveling at night during the years Ulysses was away, Kay held to the pose that she and Clark were "just good friends."

And when Kay was asked how was Clark doing in Hong Kong, her reply was:

"I haven't heard a word from him, chum."

"Chum" is what she called everyone. Clark liked that. It reminded him of someone else who spoke that way.

Clark was still—after all those years—still trying to reach out for that mirage which was Carole Lombard. In Kay Spreckles, there were many similarities of looks, as there were in Sylvia Ashley. But in the latter's case it stopped at looks—Lady Sylvia was not at all like Carole in her ways or interests, nor in her manner of speaking. Kay was. When she called you "chum," it was a good deal the way Carole might have called you "buster." And there were strong similarities in Kay's and Carole's vocabularies in another respect—both spoke the King's English with a dash of salt.

Some of this salt poured forth in a note to Clark one day shortly after he reached Hong Kong and it may have been the turning point in the romantic stalemate.

Gable started it when he was interviewed in the fall of 1954 before he took off for the Orient. Clark was quoted as saying he and Kay were just old friends and had no plans to marry.

Kay read the statement in the newspapers and hit the overhang. She quickly penned a blistering note telling Clark she didn't like the quotes she read in print and who did he think he was anyway, dismissing her so casually. Gable replied that he'd been misquoted.

Perhaps he had been, but his explanation failed to get him off the hook. After all, if he had been misquoted, then what was it he'd really said?

Well, no one really knows, but Kay herself will tell you that at another time, shortly after he returned from Hong Kong, Clark did commit himself in a manner of speaking.

"I had a feeling that a proposal was in the works," Kay explained, "when I overheard him say to a friend, 'Old Kathleen has an awful lot of remarkable stuff in her. She can do anything. Even knows how to run a tractor.'

"That's high praise from Mr. G. He liked independence in a woman."

The Great Lover eventually got around to addressing his remarks to Kay herself. It happened in the rose garden of Gable's twenty-two-acre Encino spread. The roses were in full bloom then, forming a brilliant blaze of color along the two miles of white fence surrounding the alfalfa paddocks, and the late spring was alive in all its glory with the beauties of nature represented by the picturesque touches of the pepper trees, the citrus groves, the peach orchards, the gardenias, and the camellias.

By now Gable had gotten his second wind—after charming the millions of women of the world for an unbelievable twenty-five years, a full quarter of a century, Clark was still the biggest box-office draw, and going ever better. He had gotten his second wind after the succession of post-war celluloid "bombs" and had lost the generation of fans that had grown up since the war. But with Clark picking his own stories and spots, he began to win new favor among the movie millions and was back on top again. Indeed, he had gotten his second wind.

And now out there in the rose garden on his ranch, with Kay beside him, Clark also found his second wind as the reluctant Romeo. He found the words that Kay had been waiting to hear.

What Gable had to say spelled out what Kay said she had a feeling would come. . . .

A proposal of marriage!

# 17

## *And Then They Were Married...*

"MY LIFE WITH MR. G BEGAN at six o'clock on a beautiful sunny California morning. It was July eleventh, a date I shall never forget, and the year was 1955. Mr. G arrived at my home in Beverly Hills. We were on our way to be married that afternoon in Minden, Nevada.

"I had been walking on clouds ever since the King proposed to me some weeks earlier in the rose garden . . ."

This is how Kay Williams, the former Kay Spreckels, told how she became Mrs. Kay Gable, and it's a story she has told a thousand times if she has told it once, because to her it is the most beautiful love story of all—it is the story of how she stepped into supreme joy and happiness, and found for the first time the real true love that had eluded her through the years.

That beautiful morning of July 11, 1955, when Clark Gable picked up Kay, their destination was 375 rugged road miles away—an all-day drive. Carrying Kay's bags to the car himself, Clark helped his prospective bride into the front passenger seat, hurried around to the driver's side and wheeled the car away, waving goodbye to the children. There was one other passenger in the car—Kay's sister, Elizabeth Williams Nesser.

Before the trip, Clark had sent his very close friend of many years, Al Menasco, a retired automobile dealer, and his wife, on a dry run to Minden. Al phoned back that all was well—no obstacles such as road hazards, mobs gathered at the marriage license bureau, or other encumbrances to the elopement.

"Mr. G," related Kay, "is noted for his punctuality. Hot or cold he was going to meet his old chum in Minden by 5:15. I've had faster rides in my life, but not many. He slowed down once when my bottle of liquid hair net exploded right under the seat and spoiled my make-up case.

"As we approached Minden, my sister wanted to freshen up before facing the ordeal. And so did I. My dream man drove off the road a few feet and pointed to a stream and a clump of trees with the pleased gestures of a man presenting us with the Presidential suite at the Waldorf."

Gable's idea didn't go over.

"Well," said Elizabeth in disgust, "I'm not going to scrub myself in a babbling brook. We'll go to the motel."

Clark demurred. He was afraid they'd be recognized. But Elizabeth was adamant.

"So we decided," Kay said, "that Mr. G and I could impersonate an elderly couple bent over with arthritis. My soon-to-be husband threw himself into the role with the gusto of a Lon Chaney."

Elizabeth walked into the motel ahead of Clark and Kay.

"My mother and father," she told the clerk, "wish two rooms in order to clean up before traveling further." Then in an aside to her sister, Elizabeth said, "It isn't too late to change your mind, Kay."

Clark and Kay met the Menascos right on schedule and obtained a license quietly and without setting off any telegraphic flashes to alert the rest of the world.

"We were on the steps of the Justice of the Peace's yellow stucco cottage five minutes to six," Kay related. "The cottage was covered with rambling roses, Mr. G's favorite flower. I considered it a good omen. I don't remember much about the ceremony and I don't know who was shaking the most, the Great Man or myself."

Manasco had rented a small plane, and after the ceremony he flew Clark and Kay and the rest of the small wedding party to a landing near St. Helena, where the bride and groom found themselves in a quaint old house in Jack London's Valley of the Moon. Everything was in readiness for the newlyweds—a beautiful wedding cake, a jeroboam of champagne, cold roast duck, everything the King liked, including pickles and potato salad.

"We had our wedding supper alone," said Kay, "after we phoned Joan and Bunker"—Adolph 3rd's nickname. Little Joan, who was four then, announced jubilantly to Clark:

"Hi there, Mr. G. Bunker and I just heard over the television that Judge Fisher married Ma."

Then Clark talked with Bunker in the same affectionate way he had spoken to Joan. Clark was crazy about the kids—in fact, he was crazy about all kids. When he was motorcycling around the countryside of California after the war, he spent hours at a time sitting and talking cycling with teenagers. He had a particularly soft spot in his heart for the neighboring small fry who loved to congregate at the Gable ranch pool. When Gable was asked about his open-house policy for these kids he responded in gruff embarrassment:

"They're just the neighborhood kids, who don't have pools of their own—and so long as they behave and don't get drowned they can stay."

After five serene and beautiful days, Clark asked his bride:

"Kathleen, where do you want to go on your honeymoon? Europe? South America? Mexico?"

"Pa," Kay smiled, "Let's go home."

She was referring to the rolling Gable ranch in the foothills of the heavenly San Fernando Valley, where Clark had lived for seventeen years—and Kay knew he loved this "home" more than any place in the world.

But Clark, according to Kay, was "a wonderfully unselfish man," and several days after they returned home he said to her:

"We can sell the ranch, Kathleen. We can buy a house in Bel-Air or Beverly Hills. I want you to be happy."

Kay was touched, but she knew that Clark was merely thinking of her own happiness, and was apprehensive about living on the ranch, where he thought Kay would be haunted by the ghost of Carole Lombard, as Lady Sylvia had been.

"You love the ranch, Pa," Kay said. "I love the ranch. It's an ideal place to bring up the children. Let's not think of moving."

The house, all white brick, was still furnished in Early American and with the fine antiques which Clark and Carole had bought in the East years before. It was a man's house, with its pewter mugs, bronze, coal-oil lamps, sporting prints, and sturdy furniture. Kay added gay draperies and flowers. (Long gone were the touches that Sylvia had imported.)

Upstairs were the three bedrooms and downstairs were the kitchen, the dining room—a sumptuous place with huge fireplace and bar—the living room, Clark's study, and his gun room. But it stopped being the gun room the moment Gable discovered Bunker inspecting the guns that used to be kept there. It became the den after that and the central gathering place for the family in the early evening.

"The children would have dinner on their little desks with Patches and Pretty, their lovebirds, sneaking crumbs, and Rip, the hunting dog Clark gave them, standing by impatiently for a handout."

Clark's fondness for animals was legendary in Hollywood. On his fifty-fourth birthday, Grace Kelly sent him a shaggy burro, named Baba after a native they had been amused with during their African adventure in *Mogambo*. Clark put the burro out to pasture on his ranch and he became a standard fixture, along with Silver Blacky, another burro Gable got.

Gable's fondness for animals also extended to horses. He had a stable of them, but when he went off into the Army Air Corps in World War II he closed the barns down and sent the horses over to his friend, Howard Strickling, the MGM publicity director. Strickling continued to stable the horses in the ensuing years.

After Clark and Kay came to live on the ranch, the children were put up with their nurse into one of the two guest cottages on the grounds. The cottages were complete living quarters, even with their own kitchens. But the early evening hours were for the children and they were spent with their mother and stepfather, whom they called "Mr. G" or "Pa."

"They simply worshipped him," Kay said, as she told of how fond Clark himself was of children.

"When I renewed my friendship with Mr. G following my divorce from Adolph Spreckels, some of my friends warned me, 'He'll never propose, Kay. Your children will frighten him away.' They pointed out that Clark had never had any children of his own and at this adult stage of his life probably hated them. Nothing could be further from the truth. He loved them."

Kay related how the children, particularly Bunker in this case, were stirred by their stepfather's movie loves.

"When Bunker would see a picture of Clark with Jane Russell, with whom he starred in *The Tall Men*, with Susan Hayward, who was with him in *Soldier of Fortune*, or with Eleanor Parker, who played with him in *The King and Four Queens*, he'd cut it out and proudly exhibit it to his schoolmates. 'Pa has so many girls,' he would say, pleased as Punch."

Clark and Kay spent their days quietly on the ranch. Like Clark, Kay did not believe in large parties and seldom invited more than eight guests for dinner. Life on the ranch was leisurely and only when Clark was working on a film was there any real early morning stirring—when he himself would arise at around five-thirty. When he wasn't working, he'd stay in bed until seven, or sometimes perhaps get up a little earlier.

Kay told of his routine.

"His breakfast varied little month in and month out: coffee and grapefruit. He limited himself to one cup of coffee a day and had that cup for breakfast. After breakfast he read the newspapers and conferred with his secretary and friend, Jean Garceau.

"The children would drop in to say goodbye on their way to the school bus. Mr. G then would check with his two gardeners and spend the rest of the morning with them, plowing, planting, pruning, watering, and painting fences. I gave him a new tractor the Christmas after we were married and you would have thought I had presented him with Fort Knox.

"We lunched on trays around two o'clock, by the pool, or on the lazy rocking-chair porch. The afternoons, while I was arranging flowers or working on my scrapbooks, he would spend in his study making business phone calls, discussing films with his writers and directors, or reading scripts.

"At five-thirty we'd gather with the kids in the den. And while they had their dinner we'd have our cocktails and nibble on cheese and crackers. While I'd work on petit point slippers for Clark and the kids, they'd watch television. Usually we'd have a game of bingo with Joan and Bunker and the nurse before they'd leave for their cottage.

"Before we'd have dinner we'd walk over to the children's cottage and listen to their prayers. After dinner we'd look at fights or special programs on our color TV set. Sometimes, but not often, I could persuade Mr. G to run one of his old pictures on his projection machine."

Clark had bought reels of almost all of the movies he had made from the studios—but he had never gotten his greatest one, *Gone With the Wind*. The reason was simple enough as Gable explained it:

"They wanted $3,200 for it—and that was just too much money to pay."

Kay said that after the picture she would try to tease Clark "into telling me some tasty morsels about his former leading ladies, but I might as well have banged my head against a stone wall. He simply refused to gossip. He'd break into that schoolboy grin that I found so irresistible and say, 'She's a fine girl. A fine girl.' That's the only thing I didn't like about my remarkable husband, for I'm a gal who likes a bit of gossip, now and then."

Clark had absolutely no conceit about his acting.

"Make like a great lover," Kay would goad him.

Clark would give Kay a smirk.

Once a magazine writer had asked Clark, "How does it feel, Mr. Gable, to be the screen's Great Lover?" Clark gave her a quizzical look to see if she was kidding, and answered, "It's a living."

Although Clark was a warm and friendly and charming and personable person, he wasn't very social-minded. But to please Kay, he would occasionally go to a party or a premiere. But there weren't too many.

Clark took Kay to the premiere of *Giant* at Grauman's Chinese Theatre one night.

"Pa looked elegant in his dinner jacket and liked the picture tremendously," Kay said. "But the best part of the evening to me was when we got home and he began reminiscing about the exciting world premiere of *Gone With the Wind* in Atlanta when an estimated 10,000 people waited hours for Carole Lombard, Vivien Leigh, and him at the airport. They had to have a motorcycle escort to get them through the mob."

Clark told Kay how the fans packed the hotel solidly and how a policeman told the thoroughly besieged Rhett Butler:

"Mr. Gable, don't get out. There aren't enough cops in

Atlanta to get you through that crowd."

But Clark stood up in the car, grinned that irresistible grin, and shouted, "How about letting a tired guy through for a cup of coffee?"

As Kay told it:

"The crowds parted like the waters of the Red Sea in Mr. DeMille's *The Ten Commandments*."

New Year's Eve of 1956 is one Kay Gable remembers with many fond memories.

"We spent it on the ranch with a champagne toast—I was looking forward to a wonderful year with the man I love."

Clark and Kay both had something to look forward to as the New Year dawned. They raised their champagne glasses for a toast. "To the baby!" said Clark. "To the baby!" repeated Kay.

Kay was pregnant! She was going to bear Clark his first child—the one gift in life he wanted now more than anything else in the world. He didn't care if it were a boy or a girl—he just wanted to be a father, now in the twilight of his life. He was near 55.

It was along September of 1955 when he and Kay, in about their fourth month of marriage, learned that they were going to be parents. The thought of fatherhood was overwhelming to Clark. As one who was never hammy, Clark really hammed it up, so proud was he. He went around boasting all over the place, a guy who never boasted. He dreamt aloud about "my son." He was sure it was going to be a boy. And Clark was certain the boy would grow up with his own enthusiasms for the great outdoors and his love of hunting, fishing, and other sporting activities. Even the boy's schooling wasn't overlooked by Clark, a man who never worried too much about his own education. Clark made plans about where the boy would study, what prep school he would attend—even considered the professions the youngster might like.

Then, shortly after the New Year, Kay came down with a virus. She began to run a high temperature—then went into a coma. Clark summoned the doctor, who tried to treat Kay at home. He succeeded in bringing down the temperature and stayed with Kay all day. Then he left. But about 9:30 that night, Kay had a relapse. There were pains. Clark phoned the doctor and told him. An ambulance was sent and Kay was brought to Hollywood Presbyterian Hospital. The doctor tried to save the baby, but there really wasn't anything he could do. Sometime around 5 A.M. Kay was wheeled into surgery and the baby that Kay and Clark wanted so much was lost.

Kay was broken up over her miscarriage and she felt twice as bad because she knew what it would have meant to Clark.

But Gable brushed off the condolences, saying, "Kay and I have each other and she's a husky girl. I've never known her to be frail—and I'm sure she'll be able to have another baby. She wants to so much—and so do I. We had such plans . . ."

Those plans included a nursery that Kay and Clark had started to build. When asked if they'd go ahead and finish the room, Clark replied, "I don't know. Maybe we'll just wait a while. It might be like tempting fate."

Clark was thankful of one thing. He and Kay were to have gone just after the New Year to the remote country lodge in the Valley of the Moon, near St. Helena, where they had spent their honeymoon. But the doctor told Clark Kay shouldn't go. Had they disobeyed the physician's orders, Kay might never have survived out there in the wilderness where no ambulance could reach her.

Commenting herself about the loss of her baby, Kay said:

"I was heartbroken. Clark had been such a proud prospective father, and I had so wanted to give him a child of his own."

Not long afterward, in May of 1956, Kay awakened one morning with a horrifying pain in her chest and arm. Her jaw was virtually paralyzed.

"I thought it was a case of indigestion so I took a dose of soda," Kay related. "The pain went away. We were leaving for St. George, Utah, that evening for the location of *The King and Four Queens*. Mr. G was busy packing the station wagon, so I said nothing about it. We had arranged for a bungalow in St. George."

After a month on Utah locations Clark and Kay were both glad to get back to the ranch again.

But something was happening to Kay—something dreadful, something alarming.

The pains in her chest were coming more often, and lasting longer. One morning she couldn't move.

"Pa," Kay called out, "something's wrong."

Then she began to cry. The pain was unbearable.

"It's the hospital for you," Clark ordered.

"Soon after we reached the hospital I had a 20-minute attack," Kay said, "and the doctor found that I had angina pectoris. Clark moved into the hospital to stay with me. I was in the hospital for three weeks.

"My first wedding anniversary was a dismal affair. I was back at the ranch, but in bed, and still having attacks. Mr. G fussed around like an old mother hen."

One day Clark looked at Kay sternly and growled at her:

"Kathleen, I have a hunch you aren't taking all your medicine. I suggest you follow your doctor's advice."

"He was right," Kay admitted. "If it wasn't for Clark

I wouldn't be alive today."

Kay's birthday, on August 7th, was a gala affair. She was much better by then, and the doctor had decided it would be all right to have a few guests over and dine for the first time in the dining room. By September, Kay was urging Clark to resume his hunting trips and persuaded him to go dove hunting in Yuma with a group of his pals over Labor Day.

"He called me nine times," Kay related. "And when he returned I met him at the airport."

After that, Clark would go off some place every weekend— and some time later Kay would go with him almost all the time.

Other women had been measured against Carole Lombard and were found lacking. Clark didn't remarry for seven years after Carole died on that Nevada mountaintop in the plane crash, and then perhaps without realizing it, he thought he saw something of Carole in Lady Ashley—and he married her. But, while Sylvia was high in the brackets of international cafe society, a glib conversationalist, and resembled Lombard—the similarities, really, were superficial.

Carole had made Gable her life; she liked parties, but she didn't go to them unless Clark wanted to go. She was always ready to pick up and go on a fishing and hunting trip at the drop of a bag.

The mold that Gable had left standing over the long lonely years, waiting, waiting, waiting to find a woman who would fit into it as his kind of woman, had finally come along when Kay entered his life. Not since Carole had a companion suited him so well. Kay would go along with Clark on anything—hunting, golfing, drinking, or swearing.

She had the kind of gay independence Clark liked in a woman—which he loved in Carole, and, once again, in Kay.

It made their life together stimulating and happy and worth living.

It had been a long, sad journey through the years for Clark Gable since Carole died on that dark day so long ago. Now the journey was over. Clark had come home. In his own way, Gable would go on cherishing the memories of Carole, but the memories were no longer his prison and the pain was gone.

The pain, indeed, was gone.

And now a great warm golden love filled his heart.

Clark had come home with Kay.

# 18

## "I'm Going Home to Kay and the Kids...."

THE HAPPINESS THAT CLARK Gable found with Kay Williams continued with increasing zest and satisfaction and their life together was one of Hollywood's truly idealistic love stories—certainly beautiful and sincere and convivial enough to put the Carole Lombard legend into faded memory.

Clark continued to make films, in defiance of time as he kept his unchallenged grip on the title of King of Hollywood. Gable was nearing sixty, and still he was the screen's number one romantic lead, and his pictures continued to make money. Now, as a free-lancer, much of the income was going into his own pocket—a neat ten per cent of every film he was making, or roughly a million dollars a picture. His masculinity was still capturing feminine hearts and drawing admiration from the men.

But the years had taken their toll on Gable, as they must. His hair was now streaked with gray and only the make-up man's brush could restore the strands to their original hue; his face was lined with the creases of the years—"character lines" he called them—and his vigor was not what it had been when he started out in the Hollywood whirlpool nearly thirty years before. But he was still Clark Gable, and he was still in possession of his guileless grin and he-man warmth which came through with tremendous sex-appeal for the ladies—even as he approached his sixties. Clark didn't look his age.

But no one was more certain that the time had come for him to make the change from "King of the Screen Lovers" to parts that would fit his acting age than Clark himself.

"My days of playing the dashing young lover are over," he said one day in 1959 just before leaving with Kay and the children for a new picture in Italy. "I'm no longer believable in those parts.

"There has been considerable talk about older guys wooing and winning leading ladies half their age. I don't think the public likes it, and I don't care for it myself. It's not realistic.

"The actresses I started out with have long since quit

playing glamour girls and sweet young things. Now it's time I acted my age."

By then, Clark already had made the switch. In his latest picture at the time, *But Not for Me* portrayed a fifty-seven-year-old who kidded himself into believing he was still a youthful Lothario. Later in the film he realized he wasn't as young as he thought and admitted out loud, "I'm fifty-seven years old."

Off-screen he wouldn't hesitate to admit he was shifting gears professionally.

"Let's be honest," he would say. "It's a character role, and I will be playing more of them. I like the idea of acting my age, or I wouldn't be doing it. If it comes off, and I think it will, I'll go right ahead playing the same type of guy.

"I have no idea if I can attain the success as a character actor as I did playing the dashing young lover. It's a chance I have to take. Not everybody is able to do it."

As the Gables packed for their trip to Italy, Clark also made it known that his attempt to be an independent producer was not for him.

"I'm through with that business," he asserted. "It's too much of a headache and I don't see how those producer-actors hold up under the strain."

Clark had tried his hand in that realm under the banner of Gabco Productions and produced just one picture, *The King and Four Queens*. But the experience taught him a lesson.

"When you're producing, everyone comes to you for every little thing and I don't see how an actor can act and direct at the same time either. So I'll just stick to acting."

On June 21st Clark and Kay and the children and their governess flew cross-country to New York by jet, then boarded the liner *Nieuw Amsterdam* for Holland. After a brief visit there they went on to a house they rented near Salzburg, Austria, and celebrated their fourth wedding anniversary. In August, they arrived in Italy where Clark was to make *It Happened in Naples,* co-starring Sophia Loren. During that period, Kay and the children lived in Rome to be near Gable. They had taken a villa twenty minutes out of the Eternal City, near Anzio.

"It's a good education for the children," Gable remarked when asked why he had brought them along. "This is a trip they will remember all their lives."

There had been some who claimed that not having children of his own had made Clark antagonistic toward kids. Now he was showing how dead wrong they were. He was being a very good father to Bunker and to Joan; he had taught Bunker to ride, to fish, to hunt. He was making him into a real man. Clark's desire to make a man of a boy had not changed since he worked on Rhea Langham's son when Gable was his stepfather fifteen years earlier.

Incidentally, when Clark was asked how his wife liked the idea of his torrid love scenes with Sophia Loren, Clark quipped: "Kay didn't mind, because I held her hand all during the screening."

His love of the children and his wife and his desire to get home to spend the early evening hours with them at dinner and in front of the television set prompted Clark to ask the movie producers to adjust their schedules on pictures he made to give him an early leave from work.

Walter Lang, who directed *But Not for Me* told how Gable had worked that arrangement:

"He's a regular guy. He's always courteous and nice to everyone on the set, and particularly good to newcomers, helping them get over their nervousness. Clark is never late on the set. In fact, he's usually the first one to report every morning. He starts an hour earlier on a picture, and for that consideration he wants to stop at 4:30 P.M., which suits us very well."

The day shooting started on *But Not for Me,* Kay was on the Paramount lot before Clark arrived and brought a carload of potato plants. She spotted them around the various dressing rooms and also distributed quantities of potato chips.

"I'm advertising our ranch," Kay said proudly. "We're growing potatoes and other vegetables."

Shades of Carole Lombard hiring a plane to advertise Clark's disastrous role in *Parnell?*

*But Not for Me* was Clark's first picture after a year of voluntary "retirement." As he advanced in years, Clark had been contemplating the possibility of ending his career, but he was somewhat afraid to plunge headlong into the idle life.

"After forty years as an actor you can't quit all of a sudden," he said. "So I tried a 'rehearsal' after I finished *Run Silent, Run Deep.*

"I was curious about whether I'd be bored. I wasn't, but I think if I'd stayed away from pictures much longer I might have been."

At no time, Gable recalled, did he ever consider venturing into television, not even during his unhappiness in the early 50s with MGM. Not that he didn't credit TV for a renaissance in his popularity.

"Television brought out several of the good pictures I'd made years ago," he said. *Test Pilot, Boom Town, San Francisco,* and *It Happened One Night,* were among them. The kids saw them and thought they had discovered a new actor. Their reaction was terrific. My fan mail suddenly was filled with letters from youngsters in the seventeen-to-thirty bracket.

"So maybe I'm indebted to TV, but I never watch my old

pictures on television. It really burns me up, competing with myself on the two media. As long as I'm in the movie business, I'll stick with it.

"Why should people go out to a theatre to see a Gable picture when they can see one in their living room for free? I'll steer clear of television just as I have in the past."

After finishing production on *It Happened in Naples*, Gable had planned to take it easy and hunt and fish for several months before looking around for a new vehicle, but in the meantime an offer was made to him that he felt too compelling to turn down.

It was still 1959 when Clark finally concluded negotiations on the film, although the actual shooting didn't begin until several months later.

The screenplay had been written by a man Gable knew by reputation to be one of the finest dramatists in America. And the picture would put Gable in an old cowboy's suit and deposit him in the wide open spaces of the West—a type of picture he'd always enjoyed.

The title of the film: *The Misfits*, written by Arthur Miller.

And Gable's co-star would be none other than Miller's wife, the fabulous sex goddess of the cinema—Marilyn Monroe!

It was a protean role for Gable, perhaps more artistic than anything he'd ever done before. Filled with the raw juices of life and rich with deep and significant symbolism, *The Misfits* was filmed in Nevada in the shadows of the majestic, imperial Sierra Nevada Mountains—the same brooding peaks that claimed the life of Carole Lombard so long ago.

Gable was cast in the role of a lusty, uncomplicated cowpoke, a rootless wanderer typifying the last vestiges of the old American West, a gutty, two-fisted, love-'em-and-leave-'em type who will not surrender to the conformity of an age that has outgrown him and his vanishing breed.

Montgomery Clift, who portrays a moody, slightly punch-drunk rodeo rider, is part of that breed and so is Eli Wallach, in the role of a former Air Force pilot with an almost pathological drive to move on, to clear out, to hit and run and never stand still as he pursues an unachievable dream.

Into their oddly off-beat life drifts Marilyn Monroe. She comes to Reno for a divorce, meets Gable, Clift, and Wallach, and joins them in a hypnotically fascinating roundup of the untamed stallions that run wild in the distant mountains. The horses are called "misfits" because, the picture explains, they are too small and too different to be useful for anything but a slaughterhouse death and then dogmeat.

But the misfits of the title, of course, are not the horses but the quartet of Monroe, Gable, Clift, and Wallach who, each in his own way, finds himself in discord with reality.

Gable threw himself into the role with more characteristic intensity.

"I could never get to the set ahead of him," said director John Huston. "He was always there ready to work when I arrived. Sometimes he had to wait several hours for Marilyn Monroe to show up, but there was never a single complaint from Gable. It took me a while to find out that these delays outraged him. He had an exaggerated sense of responsibility, but curbed it by his calm self-control."

Actually, Marilyn Monroe's habitual lateness, while it might have rankled him, did work toward Gable's financial benefit. His contract called for him to receive a flat $750,000 against 10 per cent of the gross, but it had an additional clause that brought him an additional $48,000 each and every week the production ran past the scheduled finishing date. Needless to say, he cleaned up.

*The Misfits,* in a number of ways, was unique. It was the first screen play ever written by Arthur Miller. It was the prelude to the Miller-Monroe divorce, and most important to Gable, it was during the shooting of the film that he learned, at the age of 59, and after a lifetime of yearning, that he was to become a father.

"Yup," he said, breaking into the famous grin as he talked to a reporter on the evening of September 30, 1960, "It's true. Kay and I expect a child in March."

It was the ultimate fulfillment in Clark Gable's life. He'd had fame for thirty years. After bringing in box-office receipts well over $650,000,000 in his long career, Gable himself had millions. He was handsome, charming and, with Kay, as content as he'd ever been in his life. And yet, as long as he was childless, his life was incomplete. Now the dream was coming true.

When the shooting of *The Misfits* was over, Clark and Kay went home to their Encino ranch house to await the birth of their child.

"I'm taking off until the baby is born," he said. "I want to be there a good many months afterward . . .

"This is a dividend that has come to me late in life . . ."

Ironically, and tragically, it was a dividend he never lived to enjoy.

On November 16, 1960, Clark Gable died.

After fifty-nine years, a fabulous career of ninety films, a life as the most virile and vibrant actor the screen had ever seen—Clark Gable was gone.

It was over in a split second. He suffered no pain, no hardship, no lingering doubts. He never knew the final curtain had rung down on him for all eternity.

It was exactly eleven o'clock at night in Hollywood's Presbyterian Hospital when the life of the brash but bashful actor with the jug ears and the honest manner and he-man physique flickered out.

A nurse, one of a dozen who had maintained a twenty-four-hour-a-day vigil at his bedside watched Clark Gable settle back slowly on his pillow as the fatal seizure came.

A moment before he had been joshing with the nurse, as he had been doing since he was admitted to the hospital November 6th after suffering a heart attack. In fact, it had been Gable's best day since his confinement. He had had a restful nap in the afternoon and was in fine spirits.

Earlier in the evening he was visited by Kay, who had taken a room in the hospital to be near Clark. They had dinner in his room and they spoke about the one event that Hollywood's eternal man had looked forward to with intense pride and excitement—his impending fatherhood. They spent a pleasant hour together.

After Kay went to her room, the hospital barber came up to shave the patient. Clark joked with the barber as he was being shaved. He was in particularly high spirits. Then later, he settled back and talked with the nurse. He was smiling and cracking jokes until suddenly Clark put his head back on the pillow and closed his eyes . . .

"He died as most of us would like to go," said the hospital director B. J. Caldwell.

The nurse immediately knew something was wrong and hurried to summon Dr. Fred Cerini, Gable's physician, who was in the hospital at the time. But there was nothing the doctor could do. Clark Gable, the man who had made females swoon for 30 years, since the long-ago days before bobby-soxers were born, was gone.

Now it was someone's sad duty to inform Kay. The task fell to Dr. Richard Clark, the obstetrician who had been in constant attendance since Kay took the room across the hall to be near her husband.

Kay was asleep and when Dr. Clark awakened her she knew something serious had happened. She took the news hard. She went into Clark's room.

"I held him in my arms for two hours that night after he died," Kay said. "Then they made me leave."

As she was led out, her maid, Louisa, weeping along with Kay, whispered:

"Please don't worry, Mrs. Gable . . . please don't worry. God has willed it this way. But God is good . . . you are going to have Mr. Gable's baby . . ."

A waiting automobile whisked Kay home to the ranch where she immediately went into seclusion with only the memories of her last happy five years left to her for the time being.

But life is for the living and Kay had to begin looking forward to the month of March—and to the baby that Clark wanted so badly.

Yet the thoughts could not leave Kay's mind—the thoughts of the suddenly very empty living room which was once crowded with laughter and fun as it had been the last night Clark spent at home eleven days previously.

Clark was wrestling on the floor with Bunker and Joan—and then it happened. Pains in the stomach. Wonderment over the sudden attack. Was it indigestion?

Clark didn't give it much thought. He went to bed at nine o'clock.

But at four in the morning he awakened, gripped by chest pains and perspiring profusely. Kay gave him two aspirins. Then at 8:15 A.M. when he felt no better, he got up and dressed.

"He just sat there helpless and I called the doctor," Kay recalled.

The doctor took one look and called a fire department rescue squad and ambulance.

And then—the shocking news that Clark Gable had suffered coronary thrombosis. But doctors were hopeful for Clark improved steadily, day by day.

President Eisenhower, who had received Clark and Kay at the White House in 1958, wired Clark advice on how to beat the ailment, as the Chief Executive himself had done a few years before.

Clark was greatly encouraged.

Then, suddenly, on the night of November 16th, Death, the silent visitor, called to write a final fadeout and the inevitable . . . *The End.*

# 19

## *The King Is Dead, Long Live the King!*

stars of Hollywood gathered to pay their final respects to the greatest movie idol of all time.

"If anything ever happens to me," Clark once said, "don't let them make a circus out of it."

But Clark had underestimated the world to which he had played his heart out—no one could, no one did mar the dignity and solemnity of the occasion as Clark Gable's body was put to rest in Forest Lawn Memorial Park, in the crypt beside Carole Lombard. Kay herself agreed to the burial arrangement, and a third crypt, bought several years ago for Kay, adjoins Clark's and Carole's.

Clark Gable's death stunned the nation as has the death of no other American figure in the entertainment world. The nation had mourned Will Rogers as a personal friend, and Rudolph Valentino as the symbol of a virile life tragically struck down in its prime.

But with Gable, it was different. It was all that—but it was something else. It was the death of the deathless; the flickering-out of what had seemed an immortal flame. For while Rogers and Valentino were many things to many people, it was as though Gable was all things to all people. Men, women, and children everywhere had an emotional investment in this big, seemingly ageless slab of exciting, stand-up guy.

And yet, the mournful pall that spread with the news was something tempered because people knew that Gable, who knew how to live, knew how to die, too. Instinctively, they knew that Gable would go to his death with courage, dignity, and, perhaps, a quip to eternity not to bungle it. It was part of his nature to do things manfully—straight and clean and true.

Gable is dead. But his legend, begun long before in the swagger of Rhett Butler, in the courage of combat missions in World War II, in a thousand incidents, off-screen and on that stamped him as every inch a man, continues.

It was the end of an era. Movies were not what they had once been—but Gable was still king. There were few "sure things in picture making—but Gable was one of them to the end. The comet that flashed across the Hollywood skies never lost its luster, its brilliance never dimmed. It rushed to eternity burning as brightly as ever.

And so the heroic figure of a unique part of the American tradition is gone.

Clark Gable is gone. "The King" is gone. The larger-than-life grinning, boyish giant of a man who stole his way into a million hearts and lifted them and gave his America a dream is gone.

He's gone but the legend of Clark Gable lives on.

As long as one movie house remains standing in the land, Clark Gable will be remembered.

As long as the imagination of man can be stirred by greatness, Clark Gable will be remembered.

As long as one small boy can look up at a man and see a hero, and say to himself "I want to be like him," Clark Gable will be remembered.

Others will come along and ride a bus along a dark and dusty road as Gable did in *It Happened One Night*. Others will zoom through the sky or lead a shipboard mutiny or wildcat for oil or rope a wild stallion in a sun-baked mountain valley or swing and drink and fight and roar through life, but the grin won't be the same, the face not quite as tanned and leathery, the swagger not as manly, the roar not as loud, the unconcealed love of life not quite as overpowering.

There was only one Clark Gable and we shall not see his kind again.

The King is dead—long live the King. . . .

# 20

## *It's a Boy!*

CLARK GABLE IS DEAD, BUT he lives on now, not only in memory but in his infant son, born to Kay Gable on March 20, 1961.

The most famous baby of the hour—Clark Gable's first-born—came into the world at 7:48 A.M. in Hollywood's Presbyterian Hospital. It was the same hospital in which Clark had died.

When Kay entered the hospital late Saturday night, March 18th, the baby almost came then, although the mother could not have had it through normal delivery. The doctor had warned that it would have to be a Caesarean section. What had happened was that when Kay walked into the hospital she was gripped by the memories, the terrible, sad memories of that November 16th early-morning when her beloved Clark died; she collapsed. Doctors hurried to her side and carried her up to her room.

Up there, more terrible, sad memories. The room was two stories above the one in which Clark had gasped his last breath on earth. But the room looked the same to Kay.

"In the room, just two floors above Clark," Kay said, "I just couldn't take it—I fell apart. It looked like the baby might come anytime."

So they prepared Kay for surgery. But pills given to Kay when the danger signs first flashed, helped slow her down. Soon she was fine again.

It wasn't until the following Monday morning, then, that Kay was wheeled into the operating room to give birth to a healthy eight-pound boy.

"He looks just like his father," Kay wept later when the nurse brought the baby into the room. "I hope Pappy is smiling up there. . . ."

Kay added: "There's only one difference—his ears aren't as big as his Pappy's."

Just before Kay left for the ranch with her son, he received his first letter, and also a gift—the Academy Award "Oscar" Clark had won for *It Happened One Night*.

They came from Richard Lang, son of Fieldsie and Walter Lang—Richard was Clark's godson. The King had given him the trophy when he was just a tot. Dick had visited Gable at the ranch, shortly after Carole had died, and had gaped at the Oscar, fascinated. "Here—it's yours," Clark said.

Now Dick, at 21, returned the Oscar—and the warm affection that had accompanied it. His letter said, in part:

. . . I grew up with this Oscar and it has meant a great deal to me. Through having it, I have found out what it really symbolized. Now keep it and treasure it, and it may ignite something in you.

But it is only in your possession. The real Oscar is *his* alone forever from all those people who gave it to him with supreme thanks for giving us part of himself.

The sermon is over. Just be as humble and compassionate as you can. . . .

The long enduring dream of Clark Gable had now come true. He has passed on his legacy to John Clark Gable.

Perhaps some day the newborn boy will read Kipling's immortal words:

If you can fill the unforgiving minute
With sixty seconds' worth of distance run,
Yours is the earth and everything that's in it.
And, which is more, you'll be a man, my son!

Perhaps he'll read and reflect.
Perhaps he'll ask an older generation about his dad.
They'll tell him.
They'll tell him that Clark Gable did fill every minute of his life with sixty seconds' worth of distance run.
And they'll tell him that in the days of his life, Clark Gable, a man in all the pure and true meanings of the word, did indeed own the earth—and everything that's in it.